SOLITARY JOURNEY

FIRST EDITION · 1954

Composed in Perpetua type 11 point on 12 point
and printed by
SYDENHAM & CO. (EST. 1840) LIMITED, OXFORD ROAD, BOURNEMOUTH
Made and printed in Great Britain

SOLITARY JOURNEY

THE THIRD VOYAGE OF THE "NOVA ESPERO"

BY

CHARLES VIOLET

with an introduction by

CAPTAIN (E) JOHN H. ILLINGWORTH, R.N.

ADLARD COLES LIMITED

in association with

GEORGE G. HARRAP & COMPANY LIMITED

LONDON - TORONTO - WELLINGTON - SYDNEY

ACKNOWLEDGEMENTS

To my friend Major J. A. L. Williams, who aided me in every possible way with the preparation of this book. To John Way-Hope, Esq., who cheerfully supplied information and advice on the running of the Seagull engine. To Andre and Jacqueline de Roy, of Brussels, who kindly gave me permission to use some of their photographs taken on the island. Lastly to my partner Stanley Smith, who lent me his share of the *Nova Espero* without a single stipulation, though I know he must have had many unspoken qualms.

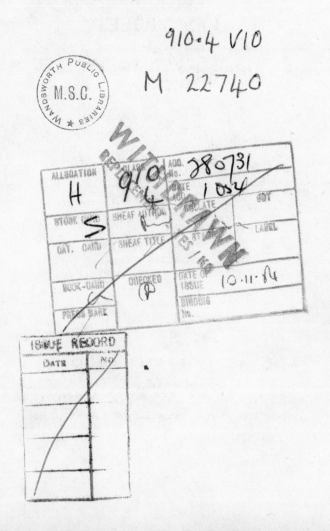

POUR MES ENFANTS:

RICHARD CHARLES AND CATHERINE ELISABETH

The Author

CONTENTS

ILLUSTRATIONS

PHOTOGRAPHS

INTRODUCTION

by

JOHN ILLINGWORTH

MY FIRST sight of *Nova Espero* was as she lay in the vestibule of the *Daily Express* office in London, brought there directly from Dartmouth at the conclusion of the first voyage—a transatlantic passage. Rather small and lonely she looked!

The previous evening I had attended, with two members of the Board of Admiralty, the reception given at the Savoy Hotel for the Smith brothers who had sailed her. There I had had a long yarn about the trip with Stanley Smith, their father, who is an old sailing friend of mine.

Two years later she crossed the Atlantic again with Charles Violet, the present author, as crew. The third voyage about which he is to tell you was accomplished single-handed, and it was when the *Nova Espero* called at Malta that I met the author and renewed acquaintance with *Nova Espero* and had a sail in her.

I am glad to write a foreword to SOLITARY JOURNEY because, apart from it being a jolly good yarn, I find it notable for a number of reasons, which I am convinced will make the book particularly interesting both to sailing men and to the reading public generally.

There is always something attractive about an adventure embarked on despite slender resources, and especially so when it is brought to a successful conclusion. This tale certainly qualifies for attention on this score. To those of us who take a great deal of trouble with fitting out and equipment, and feel it almost our duty not to spare expense when it is a matter of making a yacht efficient, it will be a matter of amazement to find how much was achieved in *Nova Espero* with so little.

Almost without charts, and without a spare sail in the boat, Charles Violet made the voyage successfully from Britain to Malta and in the later part of his cruise he even had to sell parts of his meagre equipment to pay for the petrol required to take his little ship through the canals, and the food to take him home.

And then there is the route. His voyage to Africa, which included passages through the waterways of the length and breadth of France, took him well off the beaten track at times; to ports and up waterways

9

where yachtsmen rarely fetch up. Moreover, he made the acquaintance of, and tells us about, a great number of unusual people; many of them people of the people.

Some years ago, a few of us formed the Junior Offshore Group, a little club to develop and race at sea in boats no larger than *Nova Espero*. A great many designs, many of them very clever ones, were drawn and built to. As we progressed we gradually demonstrated to ourselves that a really small yacht, perhaps not much larger than a dinghy, can not only keep the sea, but can really go places in most weathers. Meanwhile *Nova Espero*, working independently, had got half a jump ahead of us, and was making really long passages.

The technical appendix to the book will be of special interest to sailing men and contains information which will add to the permanent value of the book as a work of reference.

I fancy many of us, when we read a book such as this, try to imagine ourselves doing much the same thing, and I hope this story will inspire some of the younger readers to have a go themselves at a game which teaches much that is worth while and that may never be learnt in any other way. But they will, I hope, remember that the modest way in which some of the happenings are described hides a great deal of real seamanship. And just in case they are not born under quite such a lucky star as the author, I counsel them to beg, borrow or purloin a decent set of charts before they start, to cover possible variations in the route.

1

WANDERING AGAIN

OUT OF a low grey sky blew a fresh west wind, and the tide rushing down the Solent, over the Shingles and past the Needles, raised steep tumbling seas. In the *Nova Espero* I followed the tide and lurched and splashed my way into the English Channel. A few hundred yards away were my friend Stanley Smith and his father in the *Phoenix*, a twenty-foot sailing boat very similar to the *Nova Espero*. They shouted farewells, took some photographs, and then headed back to Yarmouth, our home port in the Isle of Wight.

Although it was the end of May I felt very cold, but I had little time to spare for thought of this, as my mind was crowded with other things. I was alone in the Channel and night would soon be upon me; it was rough and there was a lot of water inside the *Nova* which had to be pumped out; a journey of several thousand miles lay before me and I felt apprehensive, foreseeing a hundred different disasters.

I suppose I am what you would call a rolling stone, for the lure of distant places has a magnetic attraction for me, ruling out any possibility of moss-growing, and proving a source of continual embarrassment to me. I admit it must sound strange that after crossing the North Atlantic with my friend Stanley Smith, putting up with months of discomfort, and, of course, still growing no moss, that I should be off again to distant parts within six months of my return to England. I am sure my well-wishers hoped I would take a nice snug job and settle down, perhaps in a Government office. I might even have bought a bowler hat.

Instead I wanted to start wandering again, wandering on the water for choice, because there is no better way of reaching distant places than by voyaging in a small boat. The smaller the better, for this gives a "classless" voyage, where nobody expects to make anything out of you and will gladly welcome you as one of themselves in the more intimate circles of their local pub or Café.

I was not puzzled about where to go. Since a schoolboy I had learnt, often painfully, some of the history and geography of the Mediterranean countries, and had always wanted to visit them. To sail alone has always had a great appeal to me. Lurking in the dark corridors of my mind has been the idea that out alone on the wide wastes of the sea, it might be possible to lift a corner of the veil that keeps life a mystery to most of us. My last single-handed venture, to sail from Nova Scotia to England, ended in fire and a painful return to port; this time I hoped to avoid trouble. To cruise with a companion is risky, for wills and wishes are nearly always bound to clash, unless of course you have a friend such as Stanley Smith, with whom I crossed the Atlantic. This time I left him "up to his eyes" in plywood, devising a new method of boat construction. He let me take the *Nova Espero* (we own a half share each), which was generosity itself, as the boat in which he twice voyaged over the Western Ocean is almost part of Stan Smith himself.

It was my intention to go through the inland waterways of France to Marseilles, from there to the Bonifacio Straits between Corsica and Sardinia, and on to Sicily, then round the "toe" of Italy to Greece. I then hoped to pass through the Sea of Marmora, past Constantinople and into the Black Sea. In the event, my anticipations of a voyage filled with opportunities to see interesting places and meet interesting people were fully realised, but my final course strayed far from the rough track drawn on my old school atlas.

A description of the *Nova Espero* appeared in our book *The Wind Calls the Tune*, and also in Appendix II of this book. For her third voyage the little yacht was to be the means of travel rather than an end in herself. She is sixteen feet on the water line and has a tiny cabin, just over three feet four inches high above the keel. Two square lockers and two bunks six feet six inches long complete her furniture. On top of one locker I had a pressure stove in gimbals, and so called it the galley. The other locker held the charts and naturally was honoured by being known as the navigation table. The yacht is rigged as a yawl with mainmast on top of the cabin in a tabernacle, so that it can easily be raised or lowered by one man—a very useful quality for the inland waterways. The little mizen, nine feet above the decks, was on the extreme aft end of the boat. She is perfect for single-handed sailing. Of course I realized that in the Mediterranean she would again at times be faced with severe weather, but after her double crossing of the Atlantic I had every confidence in the little yacht's ability to accomplish this third voyage, although the reader will see it had difficulties of its own, but all the major troubles were caused by human frailty and errors.

As part of the voyage would be through inland waters, sails would not be enough, so the yacht was equipped, for the first time in her life, with auxiliary power in the form of an invaluable outboard engine. Among other good ideas it had a four-bladed propeller to give a heavy boat maximum thrust without slip. It was also fitted with a clutch.

My first port of call was to be Le Havre, about a hundred miles to the south-east, and if this strong favourable wind held I should sight land in about twenty hours. During the night the wind eased and the English Channel became less boisterous. At 6 a.m. the following morning I sighted land and was very thrilled with my rapid and successful crossing. I adjusted the sails so that the boat would sail herself some-where near her proper course, and then went below to make a hot drink and close my tired eyes for an hour or two, so that I could be alert entering Le Havre, which I calculated to be roughly three hours away. At 9 o'clock I was peering ahead looking for the land I'd seen earlier. Now looking round the clear horizon not a single lump or smudge broke the encircling sea. My glimpse of land must have been a dark cloud.

At mid-day the tide took control, carrying me back westwards toward the grey wastes of the Atlantic. I'd had enough of that area last year, so I dragged out the motor and put it in the fitting on the transom. The *Nova Espero* had never before been harnessed to an engine, and I was very keen to see how they would behave together at sea. The Seagull started with the first pull on the cord and I put the boat on course before sitting back to enjoy the new sensation. The motor behaved as though it were propelling a dinghy round Yarmouth harbour.

The French coast appeared again, low-lying and grey, at about 4 p.m., and half an hour afterwards the motor stopped for lack of fuel. There was another half-gallon in the spare tin, but that was in reserve for manoeuvring in the harbour. At first the boat seemed motionless, but without any visual evidence I knew that the tide was foul, and soon it was only too obvious that once again I was being carried off to the west.

This was remedied by letting go a light anchor on a very long thin line. The anchor held all right, biting into the sea bottom, but the rope thrummed like a fishing-line with a shark on the end.

When darkness came I was able to establish my exact position by taking bearings from the flashes of two lighthouses, and this put me about ten miles from Le Havre and still on my track line from the Needles. Ten miles does not sound a long distance. It can be covered in ten minutes in a car or can be walked in under three hours, but believe it or not, what with light winds and a foul tide for six hours, it was not until the following morning that I made any worthwhile progress, and gazed with satisfaction at the sunlit cliffs of Cap Le Havre, and the sparkling sea, at last crinkled with a light breeze from the north-east. When I got safely in harbour I had a feeling of great contentment at the prospect of over 900 miles of quiet inland waterways across France. My dreams were coming true.

2

SAILING UP THE SEINE

I WAS in Le Havre for five days. The chief cause of delay was my wish to fill up my cans with duty-free petrol and thus save a little money. This proved an exasperating business. The agent for the Touring Club of France showed me where to obtain the petrol and arranged for me to get a taxi to take my cans to be filled. This I did, but an adamant customs officer said "No." He was permitted only to put petrol direct into the yacht, not into cans in a taxi. In vain I pleaded, thinking bitterly of the mounting cost of the taxi, and of the impossibility of bringing the boat round during what remained of that day. But the officer was insistent, and, after using my entire vocabulary several times, I had to retire defeated. Next day there was a fête, and the petrol depot was closed, but at 8 a.m. on the 4th of June I brought the *Nova* out of the inner harbour into the tidal basin, where the cans were duly filled up with petrol. I intended to return to the inner harbour and the Tancaville Canal, but it was too late; the lock gates leading to the harbour were closed. The prospect of further delay made me impatient, so I decided to try my luck with the sand-banks in the estuary of the River Seine and sail up with the tide, which would be flooding at about 2 p.m.

I emerged from the harbour without hitting any of the wrecks in the offing, and then steered towards a large red buoy about three miles due south of Le Havre. I was certain of not going aground before reaching the buoy as I had a large-scale chart, but beyond it and up the estuary I had nothing to guide me, although I had been warned that there was less than two feet of water over some of the banks at half tide.

After making fast to the red buoy I waited for the tide to change. Promptly at 2 o'clock the sea began its twice daily task of pushing the River Seine back on itself for a distance of over ninety miles. A fresh west wind was blowing and carried me along at a fine speed. Studying a chart of this area at a later date showed that I went over some banks that were marked as being above water at low tide!

Eventually I found a well-buoyed channel hugging the south shore. It was easy to distinguish by its blue-green colour, vividly contrasting with the sand-coloured water through which I had been passing. I swept up river with the tide until midnight, the fresh wind never quite failing me by being blanketed in the many turns round high bluffs and through deep wooded valleys. I glided past constantly changing scenery; tall trees clustering along the banks, little villages drowsing in the sunlight; cows from the farms drinking at the river's edge. It was all utterly different from the *Nova Espero*'s usual salty sphere, and I enjoyed it.

Two things stood out that afternoon; firstly the hundred different shades of green, and secondly the smell of the river, which is one you can only get on water miles from cities and their pollution.

When darkness fell all other river craft stopped, but I carried on, the *Nova Espero* gliding silently along the jet-black highway like a white ghost in the grey mists of the night.

At midnight when I made fast to a buoy opposite a farm the river was beginning to return to the sea, but by 6 a.m. the tide was once more flowing upstream, and I went with it. The river from here to Rouen writhed about so much that I sometimes had the west wind dead astern and sometimes had to tack up long stretches.

By mid-day I was at Rouen, eighty-nine miles from the sea, and very pleased with the fact that I had sailed every inch of the way and saved my customs-free petrol. Rouen, with its busy docks, was a sharp contrast to the pastoral peace of the previous day; whistles and hooters competed with riveters and hammers, and busy little steamers and bluff-bowed barges churned up the river until it looked like a tide-rip.

Away from the docks I found Rouen a charming old city, with narrow side-streets revealing an abundance of wood-carving.

At 10 o'clock the following night the tide began to turn towards Paris and, in spite of the rain, I departed with it, having first lowered my mast to go under the low temporary bridges of Rouen. Nearly every bridge across the rivers and canals of France was destroyed by the Germans or by the Allies; by the Germans to cover retreat and by the

Approaching Chateau d'If—made famous by Dumas' "The Count of Monte Cristo"

Nova Espero *bids farewell to England*

18

Allies to cut off retreat. Fortunately the famous Parisian bridges escaped destruction.

After about half an hour I came up to some vague island shapes on which were tall trees darkly silhouetted against the sky by the reflected lights of the city behind me. As I had no idea which side of them to go, I decided to tie up for the night.

Next day I set up my mast, hoisted sail and wound my way upstream among the islands, following a channel marked by a white disc. It was a very lovely part of the river, but now the wind was more often than not against me, and consequently I was kept busy judging how close to the shore I dare go on each tack. By tea-time I had negotiated a particularly acute bend and found myself facing a roaring cataract stretching right across the river. This was the first of a series of eight barrages constructed to regulate the depth and flow. Built into the bank was a large lock with coloured lights and a control tower.

While I was waiting my turn to enter I lowered the mast, as my sailing days were over for several weeks; ahead of me lay eight hundred miles of tideless rivers and low bridges.

When the lights showed green I entered the lock in company with several huge steel barges, and a nerve-wracking business it was too, keeping out of their way. The lock-keeper shouted to me—move forward. Ahead of me lay a narrow space four feet wide between a barge and the lock wall. The *Nova* is six feet wide, so I shouted "Impossible, if you please, monsieur."

He got a little red in the face and began to gesticulate, so I decided to show him how ridiculous it was. Putting the nose of the boat in the gap, I opened the engine wide. We didn't budge at first; then to my amazement we began slowly to forge ahead, amusing all the bargees, their wives and children. Having pushed a couple of hundred tons to one side with ease I shot rapidly down the last part of the widening gap; in fact I was now going too fast, and although the engine was shut off I was heading straight for the bulbous stern of another barge. I dashed to the bow and took the worst of the bump on my hands, causing much laughter all round.

I asked a young skipper if I could hold on to his barge, and was very glad to get a favourable reply, for it is almost impossible to handle ropes fore and aft single-handed with swirling water rapidly changing level.

I would soon have to purchase petrol at the ordinary price of five shillings per gallon, and one pint of oil had to be added to each gallon, bringing the total cost up to seven shillings, so considering the smallness of the travel allowance I plucked up courage to ask the young skipper's wife whether it was possible to have a tow. It took several repetitions to make her understand, and then she replied with a firm refusal. However, she then walked over to the wheelhouse, and after she had spoken to her husband he came aft to where I was tightly holding on to stop the *Nova* bumping, and to my surprise agreed to give me a tow. I thanked him very much and promised him some tea (£1 per pound in France), butter and chocolate.

My lock troubles hadn't finished, however, for after I had passed a long tow-line to the barge the skipper opened up his engines and headed for the open lock-gates. A powerful surge from the thrust of his propeller gripped the *Nova* and shot her sideways on to the bow of the ship astern; I fended her off as well as I could, but another eddy sent her dashing full tilt towards the lock wall. As I ran forward to avert a crash the slack was suddenly taken up on the tow-line, and with a terrific jerk it pulled the bow away. Now the stern swung in an arc towards the wall, and I had to make another frantic dash to save it. Looking forward I saw that the *Nova* still was not behaving herself and following meekly behind her tow. Instead she was now heading for the other side of the lock, but just in time I got to the tiller and brought her into her proper position. Breathless, and in a furious temper, I began to realize that this journey through the inland waterways would be no bed of roses; there were over three hundred locks to negotiate before I reached the sea again.

My tow kept company with another belonging to the same firm. It was identical in shape and colour, and each carried a similar crew, one man, his wife and a child.

In the twilight my bargee friends eased their ponderous craft into the overhanging greenery of a small island, and when they shut off their powerful diesel engines I revelled in the peaceful beauty of my surroundings. Evening mist lent an appearance of unreality, and the trials of the day were forgotten in a feeling of blissful relaxation.

We were all on our way by 5 o'clock the following morning, and for the next fifteen hours we pushed against the sluggish current of the

Seine. As we wended our snail-like way, new views slowly unfolded themselves before us. Gaunt ruins of ancient castles at the top of steep hills; chalk cliffs strangely carved by thousands of years of weather, and everywhere the tall trees making a background of green. That evening the three menfolk of our little fleet went to a cafe in a charming little village near our mooring place. The occupants were full of character and included the village idiot, who seemed fascinated by my blazer badge. The other occupants of the crowded bar looked upon me with polite curiosity, and wondered why anyone should, or could, wander across France, and beyond, without a woman; I had several good-humoured offers to remedy the situation. I did my best to quote from Francis Bacon, "A man who likes to live alone is either a wild beast or a god," but to this day I'm certain something went wrong with my translation for I got some very queer looks in reply.

Two days later I was four miles from Paris and tied up to the barge for the last evening before continuing on my own in *Nova Espero*, aided by the faithful outboard. After supper I stared with disgust at the river, which had now become quite repellent; hundreds of dead rats, thousands of corks, and all kinds of debris mingled in a coagulation of diesel oil and scum.

By 11 a.m. the next day I had begun the final stage to Paris, having first cleaned up myself and the *Nova*. Settling myself comfortably on the stern I leaned against the mizen mast and steered the *Nova* with my foot. From this excellent position I could easily see all that the outskirts of Paris had to offer, which was chiefly factories and wharves. With the outboard only a couple of feet from my left ear I couldn't hear very well, and so got a start when the bow of a large boat made its appearance close to my side. Standing on deck was an angry Frenchwoman, arms akimbo.

"You were asleep in the middle of the river," she shouted, and, with her head on one side, gave some loud imitation snores.

I tried to explain that I couldn't hear the hooter because of the noise of the engine, but my pleasantest smile and a placatory wave as they surged past were only greeted with a brandished fist from the woman, though I did get a grin from the chap in the wheelhouse.

Soon I passed under three graceful bridges, the last being abundantly and beautifully festooned with half-naked women and gilt. I was in Paris.

B

3

PARIS AND ON TO MARSEILLES

MILLIONS OF words, penned by thousands of writers, famous and otherwise, have described Paris to the rest of the world, and each individual reader has a mental picture based on some of these words, yet few are disappointed when they first wander about the streets of the French capital. With my fondness of history, Paris to me became a stage with its original backdrops, and from its chequered past resplendent figures, long since dust, returned in my imagination to the banks of the Seine. Kings and commoners, hunchbacks and beautiful women, paraded and acted as I thought they might have done, and for a few brief moments obscured the less romantic present.

I moored the *Nova Espero* near the Touring Club de France house-boat, and lay alongside a long, low, fast-looking motor-boat flying the Red Ensign. Aboard her were three prosperous-looking business men from Glasgow, and a young man who was soon to be an officer in the Australian Army. Their boat had been shipped to Rouen and from there they had speeded up to Paris as fast as they dared.

During the days that followed I got much amusement from the three Scotsmen. They were just like boys released from a long session of school. One evening they took me out to dinner, and gave me an amusing time, their apparent lack of sophistication making me feel older and blasé, but they really enjoyed themselves, though one suffered from aching feet from pounding the Parisian pavements. The owner of the motor-boat told me that he was taking his craft down to Marseilles and would give me a tow. I was overjoyed with this generous offer, because it saved a tremendous hole being made in my slender supply of francs for buying petrol and oil.

From Paris there are three alternative waterway routes to the Mediterranean; the first and second go up the Seine as far as

St. Mammez, which lies about fifty miles south-east of Paris, and from there the first route follows the Canal Lateral la Loire, and after many turns and twists joins the River Saone at Chalons, passing 177 locks in 180 miles. The second route continues south-east up the River Yonne for sixty-seven miles to La Roche, and then enters the Canal du Bourgogne, which is 140 miles long with 189 locks. This route also reaches the River Saone, thirty miles further upstream at St. Jean de Losne. The third, and last, route follows the River Marne, which follows into the Seine a few miles from Paris, and heads east for 113 miles to Epernay, the capital of the champagne country; then 191 miles of canals and 129 locks to Heuilly on the Saone, twenty miles upstream from St. Jean de Losne. After reaching the Saone one carries on downstream to Lyons and then into that mad rushing torrent the Rhone. Once in that and it is difficult to stop until you arrive at Port St. Louis in the Mediterranean; 189 miles of excitement and worry.

We eventually went by the River Marne route, which made the total distance from Le Havre to Marseilles 917 miles.

We were informed that all routes were closed for at least six days for repairs to locks, but the River Marne would be opened first. No one, except I, seemed to mind; Paris in early June and money to burn was their ideal, but I had very little money and a long way to go after crossing France. To save myself from Parisian temptation and expense I accepted an invitation from some friends of mine to visit their cottage near Montacher, a little village in the Yonne district.

Upon returning to Paris a few days later I found that there had been a change of plans. The owner of the motor-yacht (a canny Scot if ever there was one) had heard that an American was having his boat sent down to Marseilles, so he had been to see him and suggested that he and one of his friends would be willing to go in the American's boat to see that all went well, thus saving the expense of taking his own boat through. The American had agreed, and the Scottish boat was to be left in Paris. The third member of the Scottish party could not be persuaded to leave the city lights and had to return to Glasgow soon anyhow. I was relieved and grateful when the American told me that he would tell his skipper to give me a tow.

On 19th June the Marne route opened and we were ready to start. Objecting to being towed through Paris, I went on ahead after arranging a rendezvous past the first lock leading to the River Marne. The American boat didn't overtake me until the second lock—they had passed the first and had to come back. She was similar to the Scotsman's: forty-five feet long, powered by two 100 horse-power diesels, and capable of twenty knots. There is sleeping accommodation for six people. On board were two of the Scotsmen and their one-man crew, who was to help the Finnish paid hand to work the boat through the locks. The Finn, a handsome 6-foot two-inch man called Kay (his real name was unpronounceable), had his girl friend with him; an extremely attractive blonde aged about twenty-three. Neither of them knew English, but the girl spoke some French. Kay had fought against the Russians during the early part of the war, and was proud to display a knife handle which was carved from a Russian thigh-bone.

The barrages on the Marne are few and far between, the river being slow-running, deep and wide. We whizzed on our way, at a good speed, the *Nova* nearly standing on her stern and the tow-rope as straight as an iron bar. Along the grassy banks, spaced at intervals of between thirty and fifty yards, were solitary fishermen looking like a line of soldiers guarding the route of a funeral procession, solemnly grasping rods instead of guns. The tow-rope was long, about thirty yards, and the large bow-wave from the boat ahead hit the bank just opposite the *Nova Espero*. At this point the mourning figures sprang to life and became extremely agitated; I got a succession of curses or laughs, depending on the temperament of the individual or how wet his feet were. All I could do was shrug my shoulders, with my palms upraised in what I hoped was the true French fashion of saying, "It isn't my fault." At the next barrage I told the Finn about our impolite passage, but he merely grinned, and I gathered that it was Epernay or bust for the day's run. We bust and reached Epernay the following day on one engine. There we left the river and entered the canal.

During the next few days we got into the lock routine, with each man doing a specific job, and we were averaging thirty to thirty-five miles a day.

On the 24th June, the British left us. This business of going through numerous locks was no picnic, and obviously work was piling up for them in Glasgow. I was sorry to see them go, for they proved themselves to be fine friends. The day the two Scotsmen left, my tow-boat had a bad accident, and the *Nova* only escaped damage by my running her into the soft grass bank when I saw trouble ahead. A motor barge coming towards us rounded a bend on its wrong side. When it didn't bother to change course Kay swung to port, but no sooner had he done so than the barge also altered course. Kay did the only thing left to do, he went into "full astern" (at this point I rammed the bank). Unfortunately this manoeuvre brought his boat broadside on the approaching barge which, without attempting to slow down, relentlessly advanced and crashed into his bow, pushing her stern hard against the bank. The barge continued on its way with the occupants shouting at the top of their voices, and disappeared round the bend. Upon examination we found that only the paint had been knocked off the bow, but that both rudders were broken by being jammed against the bank. We managed to repair one after several hours of work and constant dipping in the canal.

Four days later we reached Langres, and were nearly 1,000 ft. above sea-level. The countryside had gradually changed from lush green meadows, tall trees and snug little villages to pine trees, wild moorland and isolated farms. The days were hot in the still, clear air. Eagles lazed about high above us, and silently darting over the quiet water of the canal were large dragonflies, some bright metallic blue, others striped with yellow and black. Many pretty birds in red, blue or yellow fluttered about in the stunted scrub that dotted the banks, no doubt keeping a wary eye on the menace above. Only the lazy hum of insects disturbed the stillness of these tranquil summer evenings.

We entered the Saone at Heuilly; the lock-keeper there handed me a telegram which had been trying to find me ever since the departure from Paris. It seemed as though it had been round the world.

This new river fascinated me; the water had the appearance of fine old green crystal, warm enough to bathe with comfort in its gentle current. Barrages with their accompanying locks were few, and we could make good speed. One day, while having lunch under the shade of two huge trees, a gipsy woman with three young girls appeared on the high bank above us. The woman leaning over the bank started to beg, apparently unconscious of the fact that one breast was completely exposed. Her lean swarthy face was heavily lined, and her gauntness was obvious through the dirty but gaudy skirt and blouse she wore. None of them had shoes. The woman asked me for the piece of bread she saw in the cockpit. "Madam," I replied, "this is all I have, and the next town is far away." That didn't mean a thing to her, and I had to throw it over, together with a few francs I had in my pocket. Of course she blessed me, but I had a sneaking feeling that the bread would be thrown away and that in some old sock she had more francs than I. The eldest of the three girls was an exquisite creature. About fifteen years old, dark eyed and slender, her eyebrows were thick black graceful arches on olive skin, and her teeth startlingly white in a delicate mouth. Long shiny black hair hung halfway down her back. An adolescent Madonna. We learned that they had originally come from Italy for the French grape harvest.

It was terribly hot when we arrived in Lyons, but I had found several nice encouraging letters waiting for me, and feeling content with life sat in the shade, enjoying a cold beer while watching the passers-by. At midday on 5th July the pilot came aboard, and within an hour we were in the River Rhone. I took a strong dislike to this river immediately we entered it. The water is an opaque chalky-green, fast running and full of swirls from unseen boulders. The *Nova* hated it too, for she twirled about on the end of her tow like a cork in a spate. The country around looked wilder and less hospitable, with little cultivation and only rough terracing on the small, steep hills. The tall poplars lined the banks, and in the distance was the blue-grey outline of mountains. Occasionally we passed ruined castles perched precariously on the top of craggy spurs. The first night, after a bit of smart manoeuvring by the pilot, we turned, lashed together now, and faced the current, coming alongside the rocky bank by a small village. I had but little sleep that night, for the noise of the water tumbling past kept me alert. We started at 5.15 the following morning, and by midday had passed Valence, coming up to the lovely old walled city of Avignon a couple of hours later. I would have loved to have stopped there and wandered about its ancient streets, but our pilot seemed determined to get us to Port St. Louis before nightfall.

We rushed on downriver, passing Arles in a wild clamour of noise, for the pilot kept the loud air-horn going all the time, probably having friends there. Now the country became absolutely flat and fairly extensively cultivated, with water-pumps spaced along the banks for the necessary irrigation. We reached Port St. Louis just before dark, and in time to be greeted by myriads of mosquitoes. In spite of the heat I had to sleep that night with the hatch battened down, for the wretched insects were determined to give me anaemia.

We all overslept, and with everybody, including the pilot, in a bad temper, we had to deal with customs. I had an easy time, for my papers were in order, but my tow had various vital documents missing, and there were hours of delay in the stifling heat. Eventually all was settled, and for a brief spell across the Gulf de Fos we were actually in the Mediterranean (I was happy to find it as blue as I'd been led to believe), and then we reached the dirty, oily harbour of Bouc. From there we entered a salt-water lake called Etang de Berre, following a stream of oil barges heading for a tunnel five miles long which runs under a massive ridge of hills cutting off Marseilles from the Rhone delta. After being given the "All Clear" we approached the mouth of the tunnel. I saw what I thought to be a piece of paper floating at the entrance, and it wasn't until I was actually in the tunnel itself that I found it was the exit the other side I had seen. It was an eerie experience going through; long stalactites hung from the roof, and drops of cold water went plonk on my head. My torch gave very little light in the gloom, and I found it difficult to follow dead astern of the cruiser; one swerve and I would have crashed into the slimy stonework. It took us an hour before we entered the sunlight again, by which time I was suffering from a bad dose of claustrophobia.

A short trip of five miles across the bay, sparkling blue with dazzling white wave-crests, and we were in the old port of Marseilles. Standing on top of a church built into the summit of a rocky hill was a glistening gold figure of the Madonna and Child. She had one hand held out as though welcoming all into the safety of the port.

4

TO SEA AGAIN

"When are you leaving, Charles?"

"In a day or so."

"That's what you say every day."

"I know, and I'll probably say it again in two days' time."

A pestilent Dutchman asked me the same questions every day of my stay in Marseilles; he would not understand that I hated fixing a specific time. Anyway, I had felt like hell ever since I arrived, suffering from a stomach upset and a perpetual bath of perspiration caused by a local heatwave.

Marseilles did not come up to my expectations—not bad enough to be interesting, the Germans having blown up most of the old town, and little of any architectural beauty to merit a walk in the heat, with the possible exception of the Gold Virgin. Arab carpet and trinket sellers plagued people sitting outside cafes. I used to go to a little bar called "Degustation Sammy" in the evenings and talk to the owner—Sammy. He told me about the German occupation, the food shortage during that time, and all his present troubles.

The dry heat we had experienced during the past month shrank the new mahogany cabin sides of the *Nova* till there was a gap about three-eighths of an inch above the planking. If I had gone to sea with her like that she would have filled and sunk in a stiff breeze. It took me a long time to re-caulk and putty up the space, but all was complete by Sunday, 20th July, and at 1 p.m. the same day I weighed anchor, hoisted the sails, and tacked slowly down the harbour to the sea.

Outside a fresh breeze was blowing. The sun was hot but the breeze was cool. Small white clouds in a powder blue sky blended with the rich translucent blue of the sea—Mediterranean weather at its best, and I realized how good it was to be at sea again, away from the heat and cacophony of the port. Eight miles away from the harbour lay the small island of Chateau d'If, the grey forbidding walls of the castle rising straight up from the rocky shore. From its legend about a handsome young gallant who managed to escape from its prison, Dumas wrote *The Count of Monte Cristo*. I learned from my Marseilles friends that it was better not to doubt the authenticity of the original story. I can never forget how it was told to me by a young French girl in hesitant English, her delightful accent making it all the more pleasureable. When Chateau d'If was well astern I laid a course for Bonifacio, on the southern tip of Corsica, about 250 miles away. The new course brought the wind almost astern, and I hoisted the balloon spinnaker. It opened with a bang, and I could feel the boat lurch forward as I dashed back to the tiller, and for several hours she surged east-south-east at her maximum speed, going obliquely away from the land. It was an exhilarating sail. Love of the sea is a strange, unaccountable emotion. I remember my mother telling me about my great-grandfather, a wealthy Southampton merchant, whose chief relaxation was to watch the ships, with their white clouds of canvas, going up and down the Solent. When he retired at the age of seventy he had a small open sailing-boat built, and with an equally old fisherman to help, would go and meet the boats coming into port. He used to tell with great glee the story of an earlier ancestor who took to piracy and ended his career on the end of a rope at Wapping Stairs.

By midnight the wind had faded away, leaving me gently rocking on a slight swell; at 2 a.m. a faint breeze came from the south-east and I started to zig-zag against it, but by 3.30 a.m. it had disappeared, returning at 4 a.m. from the north-east, and then swinging back to the south-east at 5 oclock, at which time I fell asleep in the cockpit. The sun was shining when I awoke, cold and cramped. The *Nova* was jogging gently along, not to Bonifacio but Spain. For the next two days I had to fight against headwinds and sleep out calms, keeping up my strength with bread, cheese and bananas, washed down with a rather sour red wine.

On the evening of 23rd July, the sea became the flattest I had ever seen, and when night came it looked like an endless black shiny floor, reflecting the bright stars above with yellow fingers. Not a sound anywhere to break the feeling of unreality. Then suddenly it all disappeared; a light breeze arrived to ruffle the sea and flap the sails. That same night I had a strange experience and a nasty fright. At 3 a.m. I left the *Nova* to steer herself while I made a cup of coffee in the cabin. While half lying on the bunk sipping my drink, I was startled to hear the sound of a shrill human whistle coming down the hatch. Thinking that someone had boarded me from a small boat I hastened on deck, but not a soul was to be seen. Then as I turned to go below again I saw a fast motor-boat hurtling towards me out of the darkness and only about a hundred and fifty yards away. I jammed the tiller hard over and just managed to avoid her. Not a single light was visible on the craft, which I concluded must have been a tobacco smuggler, and the *Nova*, I regret to say, had no lights either. I pondered on that odd warning which had undoubtedly saved the *Nova* if not my life.

In the morning towering cumulus clouds began marching towards me from the horizon with the relentless motion of Frankenstein monsters. The sky gradually lost its pleasant hue and became covered with a metallic steel-grey cloud, relieved here and there with little white powder-puffs looking like ack-ack shell-bursts. Up till 3 p.m. there had been no wind, then without any warning it whipped up fiercely from the south. I had been expecting something unpleasant to happen, and had lowered the mainsail, but the weight of wind was too much for even the jib and mizen, and I lay to a sea-anchor. To the east and south lightning flashed across the sky, heralding a black, heavy, oily-looking cloud which mounted rapidly and soon covered its steel-grey precursor. Several times I saw jagged forks of lightning touch the sea, and became badly frightened, thinking that there was a good chance of the boat being struck. The noise of the thunder also seeped away my morale, and I longed for these furious elements to depart and leave me in peace. I acted the ostrich, and buried my head in a book down below. So enthralling was the story (*Venture to the Interior*, by L. Van der Post) that I soon forgot my own petty troubles in the author's tragic exploits up the Milanje mountain, where one of his companions lost his life trying to cross a raging torrent. By the time I had finished a chapter the wind had lessened considerably, leaving only a steep, awkward sea, making the motion of the boat extremely uncomfortable. At 7 p.m. I had all sail set to a fresh south wind and was once more making good progress towards Bonifacio. Having been out of sight of land for four days I took two sun sights the next morning to check with the latitude sights I'd obtained from Polaris during the night. When it showed that I was further from Corsica than when I left port I gave an audible groan. It wasn't until I'd been through the calculations twice that I found that I'd made the same stupid mistake in each, and was really well on the way. I estimated that if the wind held I should sight land some time in the evening.

As the *Nova* sailed herself the rest of the day I caught up with my arrears of sleep. At 7 o'clock in the evening I came on deck much refreshed, and gazing ahead had the thrill of making out a shadowy headland; within an hour the peaks of distant mountains could be seen rising out of an evening mist. It is difficult, if not impossible, for anyone unversed in the mysteries of psychology to explain just why the finding of an island you have hoped to reach in a small boat, propelled only by the wind, should bring such an extraordinary feeling of satisfaction. There is nothing else in the world that gives such a sense of accomplishment.

Watching the mountains fold into the night, and a lighthouse blink its warning on the Sanguinaires rocks, I thought of Robert Service's lines:

> *Have you stood where the silences brood*
> *And the cast of horizons begin,*
> *At the dawn of the day to behold far away*
> *The goal you would strive for and win?*
> *Yet Ah! in the night when you gain the height*
> *With the vast pool of Heaven star spawned,*
> *Afar and agleam like a valley of dream*
> *Still mocks you a Land of Beyond.*

Darker than the darkness of night loomed the land ahead; the huge shapeless anonymity of it made me feel inadequate and unfitted to close the ever-narrowing gap that lay between us. A tenseness settled upon me and I wished for the help of daylight. I was much further to the north of the island than I had intended, and had no chart of this section, yet in spite of my feelings and in spite of the risk I felt compelled to go close in. Soon I saw an island or a headland not more than three hundred yards away, and when I heard the distant roar of surf breaking on the rocks I shook off the spell and altered course to the south.

For the second time I fell asleep in the cockpit. This time it was with nearly fatal results. It must have been the noise of the surf that woke me up, for when I gathered my wits I found the boat under a cliff which towered above into the gloom. The phosphorescent gleam of the breakers at its foot was clearly visible. There was not a breath of wind to help, so, realising that it would only be a matter of moments before we struck, I panicked, grabbed an oar, and tried to crawl off with that, but all I did was to describe a circle back to the original danger spot. Calmer now, after that furious burst of useless effort, I seized the outboard, slung it on the stern, turned on the tap, pulled the cord, and breathed a deep sigh of relief when it started first pull and pushed me resolutely away from danger. With the cliff once more merging into the night I said, raising my voice above the noise of the engine, "Charles, you are a bloody fool."

The dawn came slowly, tinting the mountain peaks mauve against the lightening sky. The wild grandeur of the island was breathtaking. It looked at that moment part of a newly created world that hadn't been rounded off by the smoothing hand of time; then I caught a whiff of the perfume of the place, a heady sweet-smelling wood smoke, and as it grew lighter I could see that all the lower slopes of the mountain were covered in a kind of scrub cedar. On the more gentle slopes tiny, lovely cottages were dotted at random, with grey wisps of smoke already coming from the chimneys. Early risers these Corsicans.

The wind returned by breakfast time, a fresh north-westerly mistral to which, feeling braver now in daylight, I hoisted the spinnaker. I enjoyed that fast sail down the coast. I passed a tall lighthouse standing at the end of a line of wicked-looking rocks a mile out to sea, and was glad I hadn't made my landfall around there. Coming at last towards the Bonifacio Straits I was now able to check my position from the chart. In a large indentation of land I saw some houses standing on a cliff, but looking closely I couldn't see a sign of a harbour, so decided it was not Bonifacio and carried on round the southern tip. Ahead lay a chain of islands stretching right across to Sardinia, whose misty outline I could just make out. Passing another lighthouse high up on a cliff I looked it up on the chart. No doubt of it, I had passed the port of Bonifacio. Hurriedly I lowered the spinnaker and hoisted the jib, and then had to tack back against wind and a large sea.

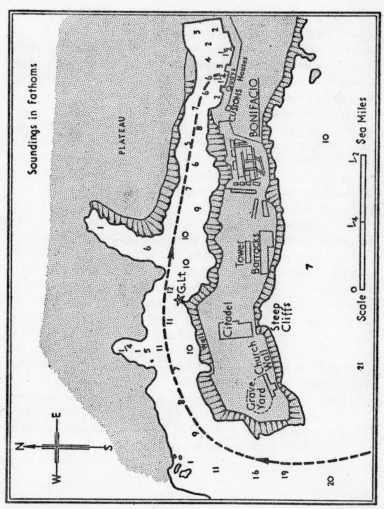

Soundings in Fathoms

BONIFACIO
HARBOUR

33

With some misgivings I worked my way back towards the group of houses I had sighted. It was not until I got within a hundred yards of the high cliff that I saw a narrow cleft running almost parallel with the coast. I lowered the mainsail and moved gently and nervously up it. What a lovely landlocked harbour it turned out to be. Dropping the anchor astern I edged slowly towards the wharf, where willing hands took my bow-line and made it fast. Above me lay the walled town of Bonifacio, its yellow-ochre stone looking undecayed and ready for the onslaught of catapults, cannons, and all manner of siege machines. No pretty little villas to spoil the picture—it remained unchanged after the passage of centuries. Built on a high, narrow peninsula no more than a few hundred yards across, it looked as though it must have been unassailable in bygone days.

The Duc de Bonifacio first fortified the peninsula in 1100 when he was sent by the Genoese to try to bring Corsica to some sort of order, for then it was the headquarters of pirates and cut-throats. It experienced its first great siege in 1442, when the King of Aragon planned to annex it. Before he finally abandoned the idea, over 7,000 people died of starvation or malnutrition, and the able-bodied fighting men left in the town towards the end were fed at the breasts of nursing mothers. Rats, dead or alive, were at a premium of five pieces of gold. The Corsicans have never been conquered, but several times been given away as a bad lot. France has owned the island for three hundred years, but does nothing to stop the piracy on tourists.

One man said to me, "Yes, Corsica is a wild and beautiful island, but there is a curse on it and its people can never be happy or content." Thinking of that greatest of Corsicans, Napoleon, I thought that there was possibly some truth in what he said.

5

THE ISLAND

ONE OF the first things I did on going ashore at Bonifacio was to go in search of a cold beer. The small café I went to was empty except for a very wrinkled old woman dressed in black. At my request for a bottle of cold beer she tottered from the shabby little room, with its battered tables, and went next door into a place that looked like a derelict warehouse. She was gone about five minutes, but the beer she brought back was cold. I sat down on a chair in the shade outside and tried some polite conversation. Being English, I started with the hot weather; she agreed that it was hot; then I remarked that the flies here bit; "Yes," she said, "they bite." Not having spoken to anyone for a week I carried on regardless of her reticence, and by becoming personal found out that she'd always lived in this town, and had only twice been away as far as Ajaccio, about sixty miles to the north. In the end I abandoned my attempts at conversation and went back to the boat.

When it was cooler I walked up a steep cobbled causeway towards the walled town itself. How mediaeval and forbidding it looked, and how strategically placed; only a narrow strip connected it with the mainland, and the walls elsewhere were carried straight up from the cliffs; in fact in places it overhung the sea on ledges jutting out. Looking back I could see way below me the little harbour with its fishing boats lining the quay, and the water a pale milky green, contrasting with the faded red roofs of the harbour buildings.

After collecting my mail from a wan-faced girl at the small post-office, I promised myself that on returning from the Black Sea I would explore this old town at leisure. Going down to the quay again I saw that a large black ketch had come in, flying the Swedish flag. While I was making myself a belated cup of tea its crew of two paid me a visit, and gladly accepted my offer of refreshment. Both were young men of about twenty-two or twenty-three; one, a Swede, was the owner of the boat, and spoke excellent English. I thought he looked ill, for he was tall and very thin; his pale blue eyes and fair hair made him seem fragile beside the dark swarthiness of his French friend. I was not surprised to learn that he was seeking the sun and salt air for his health. They told me that they had been in Bonifacio for some time and had only been out that day to test their engine, which had just been repaired. In the course of the conversation my interest was suddenly aroused by a story they told of a local fisherman who had found some Roman pottery in a cove on one of the islands in the Straits. Unfortunately they had very little real information but they did know the name of the island, so when they had gone I looked it up on my large-scale chart. Uninhabited except for a lighthouse, and practically surrounded by a maze of reefs and rocks, it looked on close examination as though there was a tiny sheltered bay on the western side. My mind was now made up; delay or not, I was going treasure-hunting first.

Early next morning I went along to the Swedish boat and told my two new acquaintances that I would very much like to visit the island where the Roman remains had been found, and try to find something myself. "That's all right," the owner replied, "you can follow us, we are taking three young men from the town who know the entrance to the anchorage, and one of them is a friend of the lighthouse-keeper." Trying to conceal my disappointment I said, "Thank you very much, I'll follow," but I did not relish the idea of being accompanied by a crowd.

Three hours later the black ketch moved down the harbour, her decks crowded with young men and littered with hampers which seemed stocked chiefly with bottles. Hoisting all sail I made after them as quickly as possible. For two hours we sailed, and gradually what at first seemed to be a jumble of rocks on the horizon turned into a little green island lying snugly inside the huge granite outcrops. Threading our way amongst dangers lurking brown just beneath the sea, we eventually anchored in seven feet of water, safe from most winds. There was a lovely short curve of golden sand, a hill of granite boulders, and then another strip of beach ending abruptly in a similar rocky hill. It all looked beautiful and interesting, no matter which way you turned, yet even then I could sense some mystic sadness about it. I soon shook off the spell by looking overboard and seeing the bottom as clearly as

"Wind and weather had carved their granite blocks into the semblance of animals—past and present"

The Corsican fisherman who told the Author of his "finds" near the island

Hoisting Roman amphora from the wreck, circa 50 B.C.

"Eve" and the Roman vases

though it were covered with plate-glass. No time like the present, I thought, and dived over the side. Swimming near the bottom I started my search, but got nothing except cramp in my big toe. The young Corsicans came over and asked if they could look at the boat. "Certainly," I replied, "come aboard and I'll make you some tea." They laughed at that, and made the usual crack about Englishmen and their perpetual tea. They were a nice bunch: one, Jacques, was a baker, another, Nicholas, was a sailor at home on leave, while the last one was the local Adonis who did nothing at all, and whom they called "The Capitalist."

After tea they invited me to come and eat supper at the lighthouse and meet Dominic, the keeper. I gladly accepted and stepped into their row-boat. After picking up the Swede and his friend we landed on the beach, and following a narrow track through grass and sage-bush for about fifteen minutes we came upon the lighthouse just as the sun was setting. Its black and white tower with a neat little house beneath looked very inviting and friendly.

I liked old Dominic the moment I saw him; he had iron-grey hair, a week's stubble of beard, and a pair of merry eyes which redeemed his grizzled face. They all enjoyed initiating a stranger into the secrets of Corsican food, especially one who could not speak much of their language. I too enjoyed myself, but as all the food was fish (and I dislike fish) I had to do a lot of pretending. The meal had been laid on a rough trestle table outside the kitchen door. Dominic and his young assistant (there being no one else at the lighthouse) waited on us all, snatching their own food when they could. I remember we ate chiefly with our fingers, and what was not wanted went over our shoulders to a pig grunting its appreciation on the other side of a low wall. As the lantern above us flashed its warning light, the row of empty bottles on the table grew longer, and we grew more hilarious. The *piece de resistance* of the evening came when they persuaded me to eat a piece of so-called cheese which must have been nearing putrefaction and tasted like festering goat-skin. I had to dash from the table and spit it out at the pig, but the hideous taste lasted the rest of the evening. We managed to get back to our boats safely, although someone fell overboard from the ketch after they had returned me to the *Nova*.

Dominic paid us a visit the next day, and we learned that he had been a hairdresser before becoming a lighthouse-keeper, so I asked him if he would cut my hair. He looked pleased with the idea, and soon I was seated on an upturned bucket, with Dominic, armed with a blunt pair of scissors, giving me a requested "crew-cut." He did very well in spite of a gently rocking boat and caustic remarks from the onlookers, finishing the job by sprinkling sea-water on the surviving inch-long bristles in a vain endeavour to make them lie down.

We all went swimming in the afternoon searching for treasure. A cry from the Swede brought us to his side. He was holding a large fragment of pottery in his hand. "Lucky devil," I said enviously. "Here I've been straining my lungs for hours and found nothing." Other small pieces were discovered, but not by me. I consoled myself with the reflection that I wanted a perfect whole, not isolated fragments.

That evening the other boat departed, with its crew seeming well satisfied. Secretly I was glad to see them go, for I wanted to be alone in that lovely place. When they had left I moved the *Nova* close to the rocks so that I could jump ashore quite easily.

After a light supper of bread and cheese I decided to go for a walk before turning in. The night was warm and the sky glittered with stars which gave me enough light to see my way. First I strolled along the beach where a tiny swell was murmuring, and then I climbed over some rocks until I reached the sea outside the bay. Standing with my face to the west I could feel a gentle warm wind caressing my half-naked body. Looking back on what happened next I can only suppose that I must have fallen into some sort of trance, for I found myself standing on the after part of a galley. The wind was screaming around me amid a wild clamour of breaking wave-crests; a guttering horn-lantern showed men hairy and shining with sweat, chained to their rowing-benches and an occasional gleam from terror-stricken eyes. Between the men were rows of earthenware jars which I knew to be filled with wine and oil. Above all the noise I suddenly heard the deeper roar of surf and I knew, they knew, what was bound to happen. They tried to break their chains while I stood petrified with fear. A crash, a jarring shudder, a hopeless striving for air, and then I was standing once more on the rocks with the gentle wind around me. With an effort of will I turned away and retraced my steps to the boat, but I knew now, if ever I found my treasure, just how it had got there.

After an early breakfast the following morning I decided to explore the island. Wearing, as usual, only my blue shorts and a pair of ancient sneakers, I enjoyed a pleasant sensation of absolute freedom. The sun was hot so I dawdled along, admiring the few wild flowers and watching the antics of a hawk high above me. Occasionally I came to large upthrusts of granite which looked as though aeons ago some giant had amused himself building castles. Now the wind and weather had carved these granite blocks into the semblance of animals—past and present. Without much effort of imagination I saw that morning an elephant, a pig, a bear, a dinosaur, and a dog's head.

On my way back to the boat I saw two figures coming towards me, hand-in-hand and naked, or so I thought at first. I stood still waiting until they came up to me, and met a man and a woman. Human beings in the minimum of clothing are only too rarely attractive, but these two were superb. Beautifully tanned, they looked fit to be the forerunners of a new and super race. He was very tall and muscular with a thin, ascetic face crowned with short blonde hair. Blue eyes and a short fair beard increased his resemblance to an ancient Viking. She was small and beautifully shaped with brown hair that had golden lights in it, a wide, generous mouth, and lovely white teeth. I couldn't help being facetious and said, "Good morning, Mr. Adam; good morning, Mrs. Eve. I hope I don't intrude." They laughed, and he replied, "Good morning. Should I say Mr. Archangel Gabriel?" In the conversation that followed I learned that they were Belgian, and that they were living in a cave on the northern part of the island.

Offering to show me one or two things they had found while exploring, they guided me to the centre of the island. They first showed me a well near a ruined granite hut which, they said, belonged to a hermit who had lived there years ago, and then, not far away, an ancient mulberry tree laden with ripe fruit, bright red and very juicy. Having a good opinion of my culinary art, I offered to make them some mulberry jam if they would help me to pick the fruit. Making three containers of leaves and twigs, we at once set to work, and by the time we had picked about four pounds we looked as though we had been playing in blood. After helping me to carry the fruit back to the boat, which they admired very much, they promised to come and have supper with me and listen to some music.

Once again in the afternoon I searched the sea-bed around me, but still found nothing except some large shells from giant clams, although these were very beautiful with their mother-of-pearl lining.

That night after supper we heard a delightful concert on my radio for harpsichord and orchestra, and afterwards my guests talked about their stay on the island. A fisherman in Bonifacio—the self-same fisherman who had found the Roman vases—had told them of this place. I immediately asked whether they had found anything yet, and Jacqueline replied that not only had they discovered many lovely objects, but they had also been photographing them under water. In answer to further questioning Andre told me that the best finds were eleven metres (thirty-five feet) down; he readily agreed to my request to be shown this treasure trove, and promised to lend me a mask and flippers. They arranged to call for me the following morning, explaining that I would not be able to find them as their cave was on an islet fifty metres from shore.

Before I'd finished breakfast the next morning my latest friends came swimming out to me, scorning the easy way over the rocks. Jacqueline swam under the boat and came up to the surface with a piece of ancient pottery in her hand. I laughed and said, "It can't be true; I searched around here for hours." As she peered at the bottom through her water-goggles I felt a strong temptation to slap the provoking brown buttocks gliding past me, but resisted. A short walk and a precarious ride in their kayak brought us to their den. It wasn't really a cave but a recess beneath an overhanging rock. They didn't sleep there, but in a sleeping-bag just in front of it. The only trouble they had at night, they said, was from some sea-birds which flew over when it was dark, and then they seemed to resent the presence of humans, and frequently dived at them with horrible screeches.

I was shown some of the best of their discoveries. All the pieces of pottery were exquisitely shaped, and made me long for something for myself. I was impatient to start, so we all got into the kayak again and paddled round their islet till we were facing west, behind two jagged rocks, where lay a more tranquil piece of water. I understood at once what must have happened. The ship would have smashed on the out-lying rocks but the contents would sift through and settle in the deeper, calmer water behind.

Putting on water-goggles and frogman's flippers I began my search. Round and round I went in ever-increasing circles until the rocks were reached, yet nothing did I see but fish, large and small, boulders and seaweed. The loveliness of that undersea world was some compensation, with the water crystal-clear and cool. Thoroughly enjoying myself, I started back to the kayak, bobbing on the broken swell. Halfway back I saw it, lying jammed between two rocks. It must have been forty feet down; my limit is about twenty feet, and that gives me ear-ache for days.

Several truly halcyon days followed. Twice I sailed "Adam and Eve" to Bonifacio for supplies—they donned a few garments for these expeditions in order to avoid shocking the respectable citizens. We discovered two small walled-in graveyards and from Dominic we learned the tragic story behind them. In 1855 a wooden hulled troopship carrying soldiers and their families was passing through the Straits on her way to the Crimea. In a furious gale the ship lost her screw, and before sail could be hoisted she smashed on to the rocks near the island. Over a thousand people lost their lives. The Corsicans from Bonifacio built the graveyards, and even now a padre with a few followers come to say mass over them once a year.

Another day we found a rare black and yellow spider; at least, Adam said it was rare, and he's a keen amateur entomologist. I caught one, put it in a tin with plenty of air-holes and moss, then added reeds and dozens of dead flies, and sent it air-mail to the Entomology Department of the London Zoo. Weeks later I got a very nice letter saying that it had arrived safely but had just died—please would I send another.

Then came the day when Dominic told us that an expedition from the Paris Louvre had arrived at the lighthouse, together with a customs officer. That same night I learned that my friends had been visited by the officer, who had confiscated every fragment of pottery they had found! As I wended my way back to my boat I felt that the spell of the island was now broken, and I must really get on my way to the distant Black Sea. Too long had I dallied.

Before dawn on 5th August I glided slowly out of the little bay, with a light wind just giving me steerage way. The sky to the east was faintly tinged with pink, contrasting with the still dark and sombre island. Behind lay an erstwhile paradise; ahead?

6

THE SOUTH-EAST WIND

To THE south the jagged peaks of Sardinia pointed to the sky through a diaphanous veil of mist. The light from the island blinked its last flash just as the sun shone its first beams above the horizon. The sea symphony began again and the rhythmic rise and fall of the swell. A thousand points of light flashed from the crinkled waves, and from the bow, gracefully cutting its way through the water, came a merry bubbling noise. The delightful solitude found me temporarily master of my fate, savouring to the full the song of wind, water, and sun.

I was faced with the choice of two routes, either to carry on in the broad channel surrounding me, or steer a narrow twisting course between the islands off the north of Sardinia. After cogitating for a while I decided to adopt the latter alternative as all small islands hold interest for me. However, as soon as I reached them the wind became fickle, sometimes blowing dead against me and sometimes coming from aft. It was stupid of me not to have realized that this would happen with hills all around.

The first sign I had that now I was sailing among a race with different customs was a small lateen-sail boat. Her bow and stern sloped inward, giving it a sort of "pushed-in" effect. I got a cheering "Good Day" as it slipped across my bow. The greeting also included my entire Italian vocabulary.

As I made my way through the islands I picked out the name of each one from the chart. Razzoli, Budelli, Spargiotto, Spargi, Maddalena, Stefano, Capresa, Porco, and lastly Biscia. A very satisfying cruise could be made exploring each island in turn, but it would take several weeks, and I was pressed for time. Messina in Sicily, three hundred and fifty miles away, and lying nearly south-east, was to be my next port of call.

It was not until evening that I finally cleared Biscia and then the wind fell away. The calm lasted all night, but at 10 a.m. a fresh breeze sprang up from the south-east. Now I could make the boat sail either east or south; the latter would take me down the coast of Sardinia, but one good look at the distant cliffs, rocks and mountains scared me, so east I went.

No one could have wished for a better sailing breeze so, in spite of the fact that it was pushing me miles away from my destination, I settled down to enjoy it. The sun was hot, the sky was blue, so why should I care?

Many necessary sea-chores occupied my mind and hands during the rest of the day. By the time the sun sank beneath the horizon in regal splendour of red and gold, all sight of land had disappeared.

Everyone has read from time to time of ships sailing down a silvery path of moonlight. At midnight I switched on my faithful little radio in the middle of a violin concerto. I went on deck to glance around, and there was the *Nova* really sailing down a silvery moon-path. The strains of an exquisite slow movement helped to bring additional beauty to the scene. All too seldom can we feel completely detached from the prosaic pettiness of everyday life, and go through an experience deserving to be called transcendental. This was one of those brief moments, and it passed all too quickly. Then the spell was broken, and the sensation of unearthly pleasure gone.

Three minutes later I was making myself a cup of coffee.

August 7th brought a wind too strong for full sail and I had to reef down. It still blew from the south-east. The seas mounted higher, and the boat began to lurch and stagger, throwing sheets of spray over me in the cockpit. This annoyed me and perhaps on account of the violent motion I felt decidedly uncomfortable in my middle. I went below and, in some degree of misery, lay on my bunk, staying there until six in the evening—not actually sick, but jolly near it. Then my brain began to sluggishly work out that the boat had been charging like a mad thing to the east for many hours, and Italy was only one hundred and fifty miles due east from the Straits. "Good heavens," I thought at last, "we'll be hitting land soon." Hastening on deck I saw it, stretching in a misty line due north and south.

In the thrill of sighting land again I forgot my bodily ailments and lightheartedly misquoted from Shakespeare's Ariel, "Where the wind blows there go I."

Being without a chart of Italy I could only guess roughly where I would land. Opening up my chart of the Western Mediterranean I drew a pencil line due east from Biscia Island; it ended on a mountain called Mount Circeo. Near were two ports, Anzio, of bloody wartime repute, and Nettuno. I decided it would take at least two or three hours before I actually closed the land, so I first brewed some strong-tasting herbs Dominic had given me when he had learned that I suffered from stomach trouble. I must admit they always did the trick. Then I ate a piece of stale bread with some Corsican cheese made from ewes' milk, and very good too.

Night fell when I was within half a mile of the coast. The lights of a fair-sized town led me to believe there must be a harbour attached to it, and after several unsuccessful attempts to find it, but only hearing heavy surf, I had to spend the rest of the night tacking slowly back and forth in front of the lights.

In the grey half-light of early dawn I saw that I was on the northern edge of a large bay, and not far away was the long dark arm of a protecting mole. Satisfied now about the existence of a harbour, I breakfasted, shaved, and cleaned up the boat. Next I hoisted my small yellow "Pratique" flag, and then I slowly and carefully entered the harbour. On my starboard side, after I had passed down the inside of the mole, was a yacht and fishing-boat basin. Ten yards from the quay I dropped my stern anchor overboard, then made the cable fast when the bow just touched the quay. Quickly jumping ashore with a bowline I tied up to a convenient ring. How easy it is to do this in tideless waters, for the quay is never miles above your head as it can be when coming alongside in a tidal harbour.

Two hours I waited for the necessary officials to come and give me "free pratique," but I was completely ignored. "To hell with this," I decided, "I'm going ashore." First I sauntered up and down the quay admiring the boats or finding fault, then I got bolder and made for the centre of the town. Except for the hot sun it could have been an English seaside resort. There were crowds of people dressed in holiday attire, and children carrying buckets and spades; the beach was a blaze of huge coloured umbrellas, with many beautiful girls in scanty sun-suits. Not all black-haired with olive complexions, but a good sprinkling of fair-heads. It was fun to mingle with a crowd for a little while.

As I needed some Italian money I kept my eyes open for a bank. The first one I came to made me think I should leave my shoes outside, for the imposing edifice was called "The Bank of the Sacred Spirit." I tip-toed respectfully inside and asked a sombre-faced young man if he would be kind enough to cash a traveller's cheque. After examining my passport and showing my cheque to various other members of the chamber, he obliged. It was not until I was passed a form to sign that I noticed under the heading—"Anzio." "Pretty good shot," I thought, "smack on the nose."

Now that I knew where I was I had to go and see the ill-famed beaches. There was little to show that thousands had died there. Laughing people were bathing or basking in the sun, and I wondered, rather morbidly, if they ever stopped to think of the blood and suffering that, not so long ago, had been grim precursors of their pleasure-seeking. Perhaps in some ways it is better to forget.

It surprised me to see so little damage to property; perhaps the Italians are quicker at restoration than we are.

Anzio is a pleasant town, but Rome was close, and as the south-east wind had blown me so near I felt it would be a shame not to take advantage of the fact and visit the Eternal City. It was an agreeable surprise to discover that I could make enquiries without speaking Italian, and yet in the end find out what I wanted. It was always good for a smile on both sides. Both the police and the civilians impressed me with their kindness and courtesy.

I eventually got to the railway station and found that I could purchase a third-class day return ticket for the equivalent of three shillings and sixpence. The journey took about one and a half hours through arid-looking countryside, but was full of interest with many stops at little stations, at each one of which an admiral in full dress was obviously in complete control. The Rome terminus put to shame our own drab London stations; it was airily modern, efficient, and intelligently designed.

Having only a few hours to spare, I decided to limit my sightseeing to one place and do it thoroughly. It did not take me long to make up my mind, for who could visit Rome without seeing St. Peter's? Feeling extravagant I called a taxi, which dashed me through the streets at such a pace that I only caught glimpses of other architectural beauties.

I was dumped at the bottom of the magnificent sweep of steps leading up to the entrance of the church. Once at the top I looked back and blessed the south-east wind, for all the grandeur of Rome lay at my feet.

As I was brought up in a Protestant atmosphere I expected the interior to be merely large and ornate. It is ornate, but beautifully so. The magnificence of the scene, with its entire absence of tawdriness, left me spellbound. One of the finest examples of man's reverence towards his Creator. I stayed for hours absorbing its glories, then walked slowly back down the steps outside and, turning left, sat on a stone in the shade of the colonnade by the Vatican. The Swiss Guard there, in his uniform of blue and gold, was getting much attention from the photographers. It was now 3 o'clock, and a sinking feeling inside reminded me that I had not eaten since early morning. Walking back to the city I crossed the Tiber, and found a little café where I was faced with a menu bearing only one familiar word—spaghetti. So spaghetti and something it was.

On my way back to Anzio I had considerable misgivings over having left the boat without passing customs and doctor but on arrival my fears vanished, for she was still there flying her yellow flag, and not a policeman in sight. After supper my worse half decided it was still clamouring for the fleshpots, and took me to see a film. The picture was American, featuring Lionel Barrymore and other famous Hollywood stars, but out of their mouths came Italian, a reversal of the dubbing endured by the Oxford Street picturegoer.

Back to the *Nova*, and as I had had no sleep for forty-eight hours Morpheus knocked me out like a log, and I did not wake until ten hours had passed, and then when I awoke I felt as though I had been drugged.

To be on the safe side I wanted to obtain a chart of Italy from Anzio down to the "toe" of Italy. Going first of all to a marine-looking building, I asked whether anyone spoke English. No one did, but I was put in the charge of a small boy who set out to take me to someone who could. Naturally we tried all the cafes first, and when that failed we went to his place of business. The man we sought was washing baby squid in a bath of inky water. After an exchange of good mornings, an enquiry about his English-speaking powers elicited the information that he had been a prisoner-of-war for five years. I felt unaccountably embarrassed by this news, as though I had been guilty of something, but as the conversation continued, and he displayed neither rancour nor resentment, all went smoothly.

"Yes," he said, "I was held in Canada for two years, and for three years I was working on a farm in England." In reply to a query about his treatment while a prisoner he explained that the farmer had made them work hard, and get up at 5.30 a.m., but the food had been good with plenty of tea. Learning that I was anxious to obtain a chart of the coast he took me to the port captain's office, but no chart was available. I was, however, given a translation of some of the lights.

The ex-prisoner-of-war and I went to a nearby café for a drink of wine. It was inevitable that we should talk of the war. He told me of life in the Egyptian prisoner-of-war camps, and a nightmare journey in a badly overcrowded steamer to Canada. "Wars," he concluded, "are stupid follies that never settle anything, bringing misery and suffering to most people."

We parted on the friendliest of terms, and as I walked back to the *Nova* I could not help smiling at the recollection of his accent, which was a curious mixture of Canada and Somerset with occasional foreign nuances.

Casting off my bowline and weighing anchor, I hoisted the jib and, weaving in and out among the small craft with the wind astern, I entered the larger harbour; here I put up the rest of my sails and headed out to sea—still flying my yellow quarantine flag.

7

STROMBOLI AND THE HEATWAVE

STRONG AND steady blew a north-east wind; hot sun, blue skies, broken with fluffy little clouds, blue sea patterned with flashing white horses, a salty song on my lips, and I was in my seventh heaven again. Forty exhilarating miles had slipped under the keel by 8 o'clock, and I was near the small island of Zannone and only 180 miles from Messina. "Splendid going," I thought. "At this rate I should complete the next stage of the journey within forty hours." How many times I have boasted of fast passages I expect to make, and I inevitably have to eat my words. The following midday I was still near the sugar-loaf shaped Zannone, the wind having completely died away shortly after eight the previous evening. Heavens, how hot it was! Perspiration poured off me, and to make matters worse the oily calm reflected the glaring sun and made my eyes ache. The cabin thermometer told me that there was no escape below—it was 104 degrees.

After I had lunched off tepid water and a couple of aspirins a light breeze came to relieve me. I decided to pass through the Aeolian Islands, which lie north of Sicily, and have a look at Stromboli, now about 140 miles away.

My spirits always rise as soon as I am on the move, but during the next few days they were certainly overworked—calm, a short-lived breeze, and calm again. My bread went mouldy and had to be thrown overboard. The tin of evaporated milk I had expected to last until Messina went sour and solid. On the fourth day out of Anzio a complete calm prevailed, with not a cloud in the sky from sunrise to sunset. My log entry for that day was brief and pointed—"No wind! bloody hot!" In the first light of dawn on 13th August I could just make out the peaks of the Aeolian Islands, vague grey shapes against the pink pearl of the dawn. With only a very light wind which capriciously blew first from the west, then north to north-west and back again, it was many hours before I could take their bearings to ascertain their distance, and my exact position. Steering the boat with one foot, I lifted the compass from its fitting in the cockpit and sighted through the vanes at the centre of each island, then noted its bearing. Then I got out the chart and drew in the bearings for each island. Now by rights they should all have met at a single spot, the boat's position, but something was wrong, for my carefully drawn lines wandered all over the chart. I went through the whole performance again, with the same poor result. It was not until I was a few miles nearer that I discovered the cause of my error—I had misplaced an island. Alicudi had been hiding behind Filicudi, and caused my perplexed half-hour.

In the late afternoon, after hours of crawling along like a tired water-beetle, I sighted Stromboli with a plume of smoke fanned to the north. This is a volcano that looks the part—a perfect cone rising without a break from the sea; I decided there and then that it must be explored. When night came I was still about three miles away, but Stromboli put on a display which made me feel glad I was no nearer. A low growling rumble and then I saw a glow of red, followed by a dense outpouring of fiery coloured clouds through which I could see large pieces of rock or cinder falling back into the crater. When still nearer I could see the lights of cottages at the foot of the mountain, and wondered why anyone should choose to live on the back of so unruly a giant.

A hundred yards or so from the shore the light wind faded away entirely, so I put on the outboard and into it emptied my last drops of petrol. With the engine well throttled down I edged towards the rocky shore, hoping to find a small fishing harbour. The inhabitants must have heard me, for several people with torches came running down to the rocks at the water's edge. Torrents of unintelligible instructions were shouted at me, but all I saw was phosphorescent foam playing around several vicious looking rocks, and that decided me; if I fooled around there much longer I would be a wreck, so I motored away from danger, but didn't get far before I ran out of fuel.

That night there was no wind at all, and I slept under the forbidding cone of Stromboli with its black plume of smoke writhing upwards against the star covered sky. When the dawn came the *Nova* appeared to be in precisely the same spot as where she had stopped the previous

night. The volcano looked magnificent, especially as some peculiarity
of air temperature had made its smoke and steam form a circle a few
hundred yards from the top. As the sun brightened I could see a small
port on the eastern side. I got out my only oar and started to paddle
towards it. Half-way there a faint breeze sprang up from the north, and
as this was a favourable wind for Messina I abandoned the idea of
landing, hoisted sail, and rather regretfully continued on my way.

Shortly after leaving Anzio I had noticed a dozen or so small fish
swimming under the shade of the boat. They were about six inches
long, with black and grey vertical stripes. Thinking that the noise of
the motor might have frightened them away I looked over the side, and
was pleased to see that they were still there.

At midday the wind died once more and the heat became almost
unbearable. Taking the precaution of lowering all sails I slipped off my
shorts and went swimming. My fish friends joined in the fun, and while
I was floating with arms and legs motionless they would come close up
to me; one even tried to sample a toe but got no encouragement.
Swimming absolutely naked is always fun to clothes-ridden humans, but
perfection is reached when the water is at the right temperature—
cool but not cold—the swimmer is far away from land and pollution,
the sun is shining and the sky is clear.

I was still in the water when the air began to move again; as I returned
to the boat I thought of the numerous people who had gone swimming
from boats with the sails still up, and had been left behind when a wind
had sprung up and the boat had sailed away.

In the late afternoon the mountains of Sicily, grey-blue in the heat
haze, came into view. An hour later I could also see the outline of Italy.
From my viewpoint it was impossible to identify the notorious Messina
Straits, for it looked like a continuous land mass ahead.

To my regret I must admit that lumps of iron, such as spanners and
what-not, have a habit of accumulating under the compass, and I have
even been known thoughtlessly to hang up the torch near the bulkhead
to which it is secured; consequently my compass has sometimes had just
cause of complaint and has been a bit erratic. As I wanted to hit the
Straits on the nose, I carefully checked all round the compass, even
remembering to move the torch, and then I laid my course. My speed
through the water must have been less than I calculated, for I was still

unable to see the channel when night came. Not wishing to get mixed up with Charybdis' swirls or Scylla's rock, I decided to sail back and forth during the night until it was clear enough to see. It was a heavenly night, with a soft wind blowing, stars bright in a velvety sky, and the dark mass of Sicily spangled with lights. At midnight a bevy of fishermen must have set out from the shore, each with a flare, for soon the water was dotted with dancing gleams of light. They reminded me of the fireflies I had once seen in the North American woods. No chance of forty winks that night, in fact I did not want them, there was too much of interest around me, not to mention the possibility of collision with a fishing-boat.

At 5.30 a.m. with good visibility, plenty of wind, and no excuses, I headed for where I hoped the Straits would be. An hour's fast sailing and there it was, a narrow strip of water about the width of the Solent. On the Sicilian side the entrance was marked by a neat looking light-house, and on the Italian side was a pretty little port. Heading for the centre, I kept a sharp lookout for Scylla and Charybdis, but no multi-headed monster and no whirlpools were visible, which gave me a twinge of disappointment. No sooner was I in the Straits than the wind piped up, and I had more than I could comfortably handle with a full mainsail and spinnaker. The latter had to come down, and quickly. While unfastening its sheets, which were of rather thin and well worn rope, they both parted simultaneously with a bang. The spinnaker went streaming from the masthead like the church pennant on a Navy ship, its yards of material cracking in the wind like a whip. I let the halliard go with a run and then dashed forward to grab the sail. But the spinnaker, as though malignantly inspired, now flew out ahead like a kite on the end of the rope. The *Nova* herself stopped this nonsense, for she turned into the wind, and the spinnaker dropped in the water. As soon as the sodden mass was aboard and the various ropes tidied up I continued on my way with more dignity.

Having no charts for Sicily I looked for the signs of a port. I knew that Messina is an important shipping centre, and had no doubts about recognizing all the usual features. I saw a lighthouse, fuel tanks and cranes clustered near the end of a small peninsula jutting out from the island, and concluded, wrongly, that the entrance would be on the side hidden from me. Once round the point of the peninsula I realized that a mistake had been made, for no entrance was to be seen. Turning back with the intention of looking once more nearer the land, I now had to beat against the strong wind. Spray from the short steep seas soon drenched me, emphasizing the foolishness of sailing without sufficient charts. Tucked in a corner on the northern side of the peninsula was a very imposing entrance with a beautiful statue of Christ on the left-hand side.

Once inside I could not find a comfortable berth near the town, for the wind whipped up a nasty chop on that side, and the only really sheltered place was devoted to the Italian Navy. Three times I encircled the port then, feeling a bit fed up, I squeezed in between two huge steamers, one of which gave me a lee. While making fast to a broken-down wall a gust of wind filled my eyes with dust. I blinked at the town and its milling throng, gazed blearily at the diesel-scummed water around me, and decided to get some sleep. Messina could wait for me.

Admiring the ancient vases in front of the cave

The loaded kayak among the fantastically weathered coastal rocks

"*Eve*" *catches her supper*

Life on the deserted island. The lizards share the second course

8

THERE AND BACK AGAIN

AUGUST 16TH—my first complete day in Messina. I was awakened at 6 a.m. by a motor-cycle race. Like a crowd of angry hornets they swept along the street bordering the quay, did a right-angled turn and noisily disappeared among the houses. Races are fun; I quickly swallowed some bread and jam and joined the crowds lining the streets. It is nearly always easy to find an English-speaking Italian, there were so many prisoners-of-war in England. Sure enough, at my third attempt I encountered a man who could tell me what was going on. It was a race round the streets, beginning with tiny two-strokes, and ending up with large 500 c.c. machines. Some of the riders were superb, magnificently reckless and with a typical air of Latin showmanship. The last race finished at midday, and with my ears ringing from all the noise enquired the way to the post office. I reached there to find it closed— for the fiesta. Now I understood the reason for the holiday air, the roundabouts and swings, the sale of gaily coloured gas-filled balloons, and fancy shaped biscuits, some nearly two feet square, and shaped as animals, fish or churches. In a large plaza were two papier-mâché figures on horseback, brightly coloured and gold-leafed, representing the founders of Messina.

For the first time I felt a little lonely as I mingled with the gay crowds, so I turned into a church I was just passing. The roof within was a wonder to behold; from where I sat it looked like cloisonné work, with colours blended by a master. While I was lost in admiration a gang of youths converged on me. "Tourist Inglesi?" enquired one. "No," I replied, "marino Inglesi." Not knowing whether their intentions were good or bad I carried on staring at the ceiling. "Goodbye," said another, and they all sat down round me. However, they only wanted to find out some English words, and roared with laughter at our expressions for various anatomical parts. This caused me some embarrassment, so I hurriedly bade them farewell and went outside.

Back at the boat three people wanted words with me. One, a nattily dressed official, requested me to go and see the port captain—at once. The other two were boatmen who introduced themselves as Pasquale and Luigi. Pasquale, who spoke English, wished to know whether I wanted a boatman (himself) and a watchman (Luigi). I explained the smallness of my purse and he, with gracious largesse, said, "I like the English, we will look after the boat for nothing, and if you moor her further away from the quay (and you should, for there are many thieves around here) we will take you ashore any time you wish to go." I replied suitably to this kind offer, and walked away with the official. I trusted them and to date had never closed up the *Nova*.

The port captain had an interpreter with him and the meeting, which involved filling up many forms, ended by being a very social affair. Captain Loggia ordered coffee while his interpreter friend Salvatore, a doctor of law, showed his keenness to practise English, for he had to pass an examination in that subject in the near future. Both men were admirers of Mussolini, but hated Hitler. Captain Loggia's eyes gleamed behind his rimless glasses, and his pale thin face flushed with excitement when I admitted that Mussolini had appeared to bring a better life to a great number of his countrymen. Salvatore began on the question of Abyssinia, but when I saw that he was becoming impassioned I switched on to a different subject—the cost of living, and on this we all agreed that the merchants and shopkeepers were no better than bandits.

Salvatore walked back to the boat with me; I noticed that he was ogled by most of the young ladies of the town, and no wonder, for what with his handsome features, crowned with jet-black hair, and his lithe figure, he must have seemed the answer to many a maiden's prayer.

During the few days I spent in Messina I explored the town, getting to know my two guardians, Pasquale and Luigi, very well, and repaying them for their services with Italian cigarettes and thrice daily cups of tea. I drank numerous aperitifs with Salvatore and Captain Loggia, and had the pleasure of welcoming into the port a large motor-boat flying the Red Ensign. On board were eight Maltese and one paid hand. They were extremely pleasant and generous, giving me many provisions with the explanation that they had overstocked.

One evening, after having been in Messina's impressive post office with its interior open to the skies and filled with palms and tropical shrubs, I came back to the *Nova* and found Pasquale asleep on my bunk, drunk as a lord. As I got him out he kept muttering, "No take anything—I honest man," but all my possessions had been opened and searched, although I couldn't find anything missing. He became very apologetic later on, saying, "Too much wine, too hot, very bad."

Two things annoyed me in Messina: one was the way men abused and beat their donkeys—I nearly got into a riot when I tried to dissuade a particularly repulsive gentleman from hitting his donkey on the head with a heavy stick. The other cause for revulsion was the way in which the corners of all public buildings were used as urinals, and as a result stank to high heaven.

On 20th August I sailed out of Messina harbour on my way to Reggio, which lies across the Straits in Italy. Here I had arranged a rendezvous with my Maltese friends who had left the previous evening. Getting away had not been easy, for my anchor fouled a sewer-pipe. I hauled and heaved from all directions for nearly half an hour, when the anchor suddenly folded up and came away easily—too easily, for its abrupt release sprawled me on the deck, much to the amusement of the crowd watching my struggles.

Outside the port the air smelled sweet and clean and the oppressive heat was gone. The *Nova*, heeling over to a fresh north wind, showed me her flanks with disgust, for they were covered with diesel scum. "Never mind, old girl," I said, "I'll clean you up at the next decent port of call."

I arrived at Reggio in time to have lunch with the Maltese, after which I took them sailing. Joe Vella, the owner of their craft, didn't think much of this mode of transport; too slow, too uncertain. The harbour was empty of shipping, apart from a ferry that commuted with Messina, and it was possible to see bottom many feet down. In the evening I went overboard and with a paraffin-soaked cloth cleaned up *Nova*'s topsides.

Before retiring to my bunk I had a prowl round the town, but did not see anything of great architectural beauty or historical interest. The Maltese left at 6 o'clock the following morning for Valetta, but my departure had to be postponed until the market was open. The next leg of my journey being about five hundred miles, I had to stock up with enough bread and fruit to last at least ten days. A narrow street half a mile long filled with small stalls made one of the most interesting open-air markets I had ever been in. A cheery hubbub which sounded like background music filled the air. Rich colours of ripe fruit gleamed from many stalls; ladies' lingerie, great lumps of freshly cut meat, ties and braces, green vegetables, kaleidoscopic cretonnes, and all around me olive-skinned people, brown-eyed, black-haired and vivacious. I bought some apricots, deep purple figs, pears, bananas, rosy apples, potatoes, cheese and half a dozen loaves of golden-brown bread.

Leaving Reggio at 11 a.m. I was pleased to find a steady breeze blowing astern. Putting up the spinnaker to hurry me on my way was the usual struggle single-handed, but after many dashes back to the tiller to keep the *Nova* on her course I had it set and drawing nicely. It was up ten minutes, then the wind swung right round from astern to ahead. Exercising a few swear-words, I brought the spinnaker down and started tacking. That did not last long, for the wind decided to go away and play somewhere else. For the rest of the day a current helped me to edge towards Italy's "toe," and in the evening light cats' paws kept me hard at work. The night was one of my worst at sea. At 10 o'clock all was quiet, no wind, flat sea. Suddenly I heard the distant roar of breaking water. It rapidly got louder and nearer; I lowered all sail and stood by waiting for the worst. Soon I could make out the phosphorescent gleam from broken wave-crests astern, and in a moment or two they were all around. The *Nova* jumped and tossed about, the waves broke aboard, and I was thoroughly frightened. The roar passed away, the sea became calm, and so did I. Not a breath of wind the whole time.

At midnight I hoisted the sails in order to catch any faint airs that might come my way; then I went below to make a cup of coffee. In the midst of filling the kettle a young tornado slipped down from the Italian hills, crossed the mile-wide strip which separated me from the shore, then hit the *Nova* with savage fury. Over she went till the masts were nearly parallel with the sea. I was pitched out of the port bunk and my head hit the opposite side with a bang that left me dazed. Before I could recover my wits the *Nova* was standing upright once more with water dripping from her mainsail. I could feel a rapidly growing lump on my head, but I went on deck and lowered the wet mass. Several times during the night these fierce winds tore down but now, with only jib and mizen set, the *Nova* merely snorted forward for a few hundred yards, although my nerves suffered each time.

In the next few days I slowly worked my way past the arid-looking shores of Southern Italy, with their colours ranging from the cream of quartz outcrops to the russet-brown of sun-dried vegetation lying in streaks beneath the dark jagged rocks of steep hills. Past the Gulf of Taranto, past the heel, now miles to the north, and far into the Ionian Sea.

By now I was becoming very worried about the time I was taking. Winter with its storms and cold would be waiting for me on my way back to England, for it never entered my head that I would not be back there before Christmas.

All trace of land had disappeared, the south-west wind was light and fitful. The sun sank below the horizon, leaving a hard bronze-looking sky. "Oh-ho!" I thought, "a change of weather; let's hope it will change my rate of progress."

It did indeed, for in the early hours of the morning the wind blew straight, hard and true—from dead ahead. This easterly gale broke the last straw of my resolution. To hell with the Black Sea and the Russians; I would go and look at Africa instead, and what was more I would visit some more Sicilian ports; I would go to Malta and see those nice chaps again; I would go anywhere but the Black Sea. With a hawser over the stern to prevent twisting broadside on to the now really large seas, and only the jib raised to the wind, I followed the scudding clouds to the west. As the *Nova* had weathered many worse gales than this I felt no fear, and really enjoyed the fast, exhilarating motion. Perched on a foaming wave-crest we would plane for a few moments, then drop back into the trough, up again and forward at breakneck speed, just like a roller-coaster. Twice the *Nova* failed to rise quickly enough to the steep following sea, and a small cataract would sweep over me, but the air was warm and the speed was fast. The sun blinking behind the broken clouds gave sparkling life to the blue and white world around me, and for a brief spell I had not a care in the world.

For twelve hours it blew hard, and sixty miles westing were made good. It lessened during the night and I was able to make all sail, but in the morning it fell away altogether. Not for long, though, for within a couple of hours I had a light breeze from the north-west. This was a lucky break, for the *Nova* would now steer herself and I could get some much-needed sleep.

Towards evening I could see the faint outline of Sicily, and what was even better smoke from a volcano was zig-zagging across the darkening sky. This, I knew, must be Etna, and the port of Catania must be a little to the south of it. Looking back to the east, already alight with stars, and to the heavy swell still rolling from that direction, two closely-linked Biblical quotations came to mind: "With the east wind thou breakest up the ships of Tarshish" and "Who are these that fly as a cloud, and as doves to their windows? Surely the isles shall wait for me and the ships of Tarshish."

All my idle boasts of not caring about reaching my original destination now seemed empty and foolish, and deep down was a sense of keen disappointment.

Slowly and silently I entered the port of Catania, past the mole on which the heavy swell was breaking, and finally into the motionless waters of the inner harbour. I anchored alongside a derelict-looking tramp steamer, and was just going below when up came a police launch. "Who are you? Where are you from? What's your name? What's the name of your boat? Where are your ship's papers? You can't anchor here," were fired at me in rapid succession. Blast all officials, I thought, and started to answer some of the questions. I must have been too slow for the man in charge said, "Follow me." I heaved up the anchor, hauled up the sails, and wandered after them. All the way there they fussed around me like a hen with a wayward chick. As soon as they had got me where they wanted three men jumped aboard. One, who spoke English, seemed pleasant enough, and when I asked him whether the morning would do for the signing of papers, etc., he surprised me by saying "Yes" and leading the others off the boat.

9

HOSPITALITY—SICILIAN

CATANIA, a noisy bustling town, has many fine buildings, and statues, but the main street reminded me of London, for men were busy digging holes all along it.

One particularly fine piece of sculpture was a beautiful fountain, which consisted of rampant horses spurting water from their nostrils, with mermaids holding on to their manes. (Not quite the orthodox mermaids—these had two legs, and only the lower part of each limb turned fishy.) Naked figures of a man and a woman adorned the top. I was lost in admiration when a tap on the shoulder brought me to earth with a start. A coloured man speaking most atrocious English wanted to know whether I wished to buy some cloth—enough to make four suits. While I was trying to make him understand a polite refusal, another man joined in the discussion with the usual lack of Latin restraint. He immediately wanted to see the stuff, and all three of us went into a quiet alley-way; then, looking suspiciously around, the coloured man whipped open the case he was carrying and there, sure enough, were four neat rolls of suiting. He wanted dollars for the material, for he laboriously explained that he was a Finn (his father must have been one of the roving kind) off an American ship. The uninvited third took me to one side and said, "I'm a tailor from Syracuse—beautiful material—you buy—then bring to my shop and I'll give you Italian lira—double value." "No," I replied. "He wants more dollars for it than I have, you might get him to accept lira." The tailor, fat, short and bald, turned to the Finn, pulled out a wad of dirty notes, flourished them under his nose and said "One hundred lira to the dollar; I'll give you four thousand lira for the lot."

I involuntarily shouted, "No, there's six hundred and ten lira to the dollar."

"Shut up!" bawled the tailor, giving me a broad wink. The wrangle continued for about a quarter of an hour, with many appeals to me. In the end I could have bought the lot for twenty dollars, but the crafty tailor was getting on my nerves and I felt like swatting him on his pate, now glistening all over with sweat. He must have realized that all his arguments had failed, for he suddenly gripped me by the arm and walked us away, leaving the poor Finn looking disconsolately at the cloth now strewn all around him, for the tailor had pinched, stretched and tested with his teeth nearly every inch of it.

Once in the road again the little tailor whisked me into a café, sat me down at a table, and brought me a cold beer. He went back to the bar and told the whole story to some of his cronies gathered there, even bringing out his money and waving it about. I bought him a beer and then walked out. Acting on impulse, I crossed the street and stood in a secluded shop doorway from which I could see the café. After a few minutes the tailor emerged, looked around, and then walked down the street to where the Finn was standing. They had a few moments of serious talk; then they walked away together.

After purchasing a few supplies I returned to the boat, stopping at the palatial Customs House, with its crowds of lolling uniformed officials, to have my passport stamped for exit.

A light lunch of cream cheese, bread and banana, and I was ready to carry on to Syracuse, a port I had heard to be the prettiest in Sicily. Coming up on deck I looked across the harbour and saw a man busy painting a boat. Its colour-scheme was so fantastic that I was compelled to postpone my departure and take a closer look. The design was of every colour in the rainbow, elaborate and intricate; the artist, squatting on his haunches with a large sun-hat on his head, was applying the finishing touches with a pencil brush. Although I walked round several times, taking photographs, he never budged.

There were several lateen sailing coasters in this part of the harbour, all decoratively painted. One, at least fifty feet long, displayed on her bows the usual eye, then St. George killing a dragon, followed up by a mermaid blowing a trumpet. I left the scene filled with the determination to shock our yachting fraternity at home by having a boat painted in a similar manner.

Outside the port a good steady breeze was blowing, unfortunately against me, but it was pleasant sailing out to sea on one tack and standing into the shore again. The jumbled mountains and narrow coastal plain covered with dark evergreen trees, dotted with colour-washed cottages, the ever changing rocky coastline and the rich shades of green where the shallow water covered a sandy bottom, made a gay scene, though I have no doubt that without the daily bright sunlight it would be rather sombre and forbidding. Towards evening it was apparent that I was not going to reach Syracuse, but round a headland lay the small port of Augusta and I decided to go there for the night.

Once round the headland I saw a large bay tucked into its southern side. I turned into it with a good burst of speed, for now the wind was nearly astern. The sun, low in the horizon, shone into my eyes, but I could make out buildings in the furthest corner, and headed the boat directly towards them. A sudden grinding crash, the *Nova* jumped upwards, paused, lifted on a swell, then continued on her way. I had evidently hit a sunken rock, but before I could do anything the *Nova* struck again, this time on a weed-covered rock which sloped gradually up to within a foot of the surface. The *Nova* had skidded up the slope and lifted her fore-part high and dry. When my panic subsided a little I cursed my lack of charts; I cursed the sun for blinding me to these dangers; I cursed nearly everything except myself. Then I hauled in the mainsail tightly in the forlorn hope that the wind might push her far enough over on her side to sail off. It failed. I got an oar and tried to push her back down the slope. That failed. I put on the engine, turned it until its propeller shaft was at right angles to the boat, then opened the throttle wide to make the stern swing round and force the bow down the slope. That failed.

I was scratching my head wondering what to do next when two fishermen rowed over to me. Volumes of instructions came from both of them, but I could not understand a word, and went on futilely pushing with an oar. The younger of the fishermen jumped out of their boat, waded across to me, put his shoulder on the bow, and heaved; nothing happened until I went to the opposite side and, hanging on the rigging, made the *Nova* lean my way. Now when he heaved she ground down the slope into slightly deeper water, but the sea all around me was too shallow for the *Nova* upright with sails furled. It took us a long time to push and heave over the shallows to a narrow channel that meandered through the shoals.

Naturally I was very grateful to my two helpers, and gave them all that remained of my tinned supplies and some lira. Deciding to stay in the channel for the night I asked the younger of the two to bring me out a loaf of bread in the morning, and then I went below, cooked a meal, and turned in for an early night.

I came on deck next morning to see the sun rise over the headland in a glory of colours. Turning to look at the town I could see that the port was not in the bay at all, but round the innermost arm. The town looked very charming with its weathered walls sheltering houses clustered round a large church. I spotted my previous night's helper rowing out towards me; when he came alongside he passed over a loaf of bread and I handed to him the money due plus something for his trouble. He expostulated that it was not enough, and pointed out that he had rescued my boat yesterday and that Englishmen had much money. "Not this one," I replied, or tried to reply in my meagre Italian. He raved at me, but his incomprehensible eloquence was wasted. Then he rowed away, pausing now and again to renew his shouts and wave his fists. This change after last night's behaviour must have been caused by some cronies in his favourite café, who no doubt told him that I was an easy target for some money. They little knew!

I was glad to leave this port, and sailed out taking particular care to avoid running aground again, and continued on my way to Syracuse. The next hop was a short one, and the wind was favourable. Two small lighthouses, one red and one green, marked the entrance to a compact harbour which seemed to be full of row-boats. No tell-tale rocky-brown lurked below the surface on the way in, and, aiming the Nova's bow mid-way between the two towers I sailed boldly inside, seeing on the left a quay with a convenient row of bollards, very handy for my bowline. Pushing the tiller hard down we swung round towards the quay. Then, bump! We had hit the bottom again, this time with a crowd of onlookers. Having got the sails down in a hurry I tried to use the oar to get back into deep water. A dinghy put out from the quay and the occupant offered to help me. "No," I answered rudely, thinking of the unpleasantness of the morning. "No money, I can manage." He withdrew to a short distance and watched my efforts. As the boat rose on the small incoming swell I heaved on the oar and moved her back a few inches, but then the fresh wind moved her forward before I could get the oar into position again. This was a case where the outboard would solve my problem, so I fixed it on the stern and started the motor. A few more grinding shocks and we were clear. The man in the dinghy, pulling hard on his oars, overtook me and said, "I'm the vice-commodore from the Yacht Club; we would be very honoured to have you as our guest." Filled with embarrassment for my previous shortness of temper, I thanked him and tried to explain what had happened earlier. He replied that he wanted no money, but only wished to help me, and expressed his regret at the trouble I had experienced that morning. Guiding me down the harbour, which he explained was only for small fishing-boats, he said that recently the Yacht Club had cut a narrow channel down the centre, so that keel-boats could come right up to the club-house, which lay opposite the entrance.

The reception I had at the Club showed me how hospitable Italians can be. I was not allowed to eat any meal on the *Nova Espero* except breakfast. On the evening of my arrival I was taken by the vice-commodore and the secretary to dinner, in an hotel famous for its food throughout Sicily for hundreds of years. I had minestrone, steak well garnished with garlic, three kinds of vegetables, huge luscious peaches in a bowl of ice, all speeded on their way by many types of red and white wine, finishing up with a bottle on the house. My hosts, one of whom spoke excellent English, had heard of the former exploits of the *Nova Espero*, and asked me many questions, some amusing, and some very much to the point.

The next day I was escorted round the town, which was the most beautiful I had been in. Alternate red and white oleander trees lined the streets, and water-ways criss-crossed the town spanned by artistic bridges. Wide streets, magnificent buildings, ancient churches and modern shops impressed themselves upon my memory. Syracuse the Glorious!

On the side of the town opposite the small harbour was another, more open port capable of docking large steamers. From here boats left on a regular run to Malta. I was told that the Club often sent boats over there to race against the Royal Malta Yacht Club, who in turn came to race in Syracuse. Of course, he added, the Maltese are more Italian than anything else. Remembering the pounding that Malta had taken during the war, I felt that these people must have had many qualms about the whole business, especially those who had sailed there in friendly rivalry pre-war.

My lunch was brought to me on a tray when I arrived back at the Club. There was enough to feed half a dozen people. Never a big eater, it was difficult to make any impression on the mass. After making a dent in the mountain of spaghetti, I tackled the tuna, but could only eat one of the four cutlets. Two bottles of wine were brought for me, one being the same kind as that brought out by the hotel in my honour. It was made from grapes grown on the side of Mount Etna, and the flavour of sweet grapes was still present. A most delicious drink, but it made me very sleepy.

In the evening the members made a large circle of chairs on which we sat swapping yarns, the secretary doing his best to keep up with the interpreting.

On 28th August I said goodbye to all at the Club and set sail for Malta.

Down to Cape Passero, where Sicily sweeps away to the west, I had a good sailing wind. It died away when I was about three miles south of the cape. During the night and all the next day the wind deserted me. The Passero lighthouse gleamed its warning, telling me that in twenty-four hours I had made about six miles southing. A breeze at midnight came to my aid. Fortunately it was from a direction which made it possible for the *Nova* to sail herself. Taking the precaution of hanging an oil lantern in the rigging, I let the *Nova* slip steadily southward with, I hoped, my guardian angel keeping watch, while I went below to sleep. The sun was high in the sky when I awoke and, realizing belatedly that it had been a risky thing to sleep at all, I hastily poked my head out of the hatchway.

Good old guardian angel! There was Malta dead ahead. Chortling with pleasure I ducked below and cooked my breakfast, after which I set to work to clean up the boat inside and out. My own countrymen were ahead, and there would be keen-eyed yachtsmen among them.

Malta looked very barren and sunbaked, and the high yellow ochre walls of Valetta were in keeping with the rest of the island. Following in the wake of a fishing-boat I entered the harbour at 4 p.m. Various offshoots of the port were filled with British warships of every type. I sailed about the harbour and up the various branches looking for a place to tie alongside, but everywhere near the quays was either too shallow or occupied by the Navy. I began to despair of being able to tie up to a quay, and having no dinghy it was going to be a nuisance to anchor off, but there seemed to be no alternative. Suddenly a voice, directed at a man rowing near some yachts, boomed out, "Tell that boat with pink sails to moor on one of our buoys." Looking up at the faded canvas, which had once been brick, I thought, "Pink? He must be colour-blind; they're only a little faded."

I saw the man stand up in the row-boat and wave to me to come towards him; this I did, but on the way a hard gust of wind came whistling down from an unexpected quarter, giving the *Nova* a quick surge forwards. I rammed the row-boat, missed the proffered buoy-rope, and then had to suffer the yachtsman's greatest indignity, that of having a second try at picking up a mooring. I imagined people getting together and saying, "My goodness, that chap looks a menace in a boat." Not a bit of it. Although I bungled outside the Royal Malta Yacht Club, I was accorded a wonderful welcome and was given the freedom of the Club.

Soon, feeling relaxed and at home, I was able to enjoy the rare pleasure of hearing English talked all around me.

10

HOSPITALITY—MALTESE

CICERO'S SPEECH against Caius Verres in the Roman Senate:

> "*There is an island called Melita, O Judges, separated from Sicily by a sufficiently long and perilous navigation. In it is a town of the same name to which Verres never went, though it became for three years a manufactory to him for weaving woman's garments . . . The deputies from Malta, sent by the public Authorities of their state, say that the shrine of Juno was plundered . . .*"

Upon ringing up Joe Vella, owner of the motor cruiser I met in Messina, I was enthusiastically greeted and invited to have all my meals at his hotel. "Unfortunately," he said, "I can't put you up for the place is full, but hold on at the Club; I'm coming round to see you." Within a few minutes he was there with two of his friends I had met on his boat, Captain Podesta and Joseph Meceirca. We had a few drinks with Flight Lieutenant McGarth, to whom I had been introduced by the Club secretary. McGarth asked me to stay at his flat in Rabat, the highest part of the island. Although not liking to leave the *Nova*, I couldn't resist the opportunity it would give me to see what he assured me was the finest view in the island.

Sleep did not come that night, for though the bed was wide and comfortable I missed the lap-lapping of water against the sides of the boat. Reflecting on all that I had heard in the past about Malta from Navy people, I felt they must have been biased against it by the Service. What I had seen so far had been a very interesting combination of past and present, and the island seemed to me to possess a very individual character. Mac's flat, high on its hill above Valetta, had a superb view of the eastern half of Malta. All shades of brown in the tiny walled fields, with here and there the green patches of irrigated farms. Grapevines covered half the flat's verandah. "Just lift up your hand and help yourself," said Mac. Large and juicy they were—sheer luxury!

I finally dropped off to sleep, and my last conscious thought was of a day's fishing promised for the next day. Joe Vella, Captain Podesta, and some other Maltese friends I had met in Sicily were taking me on a fishing expedition—a sort of busman's holiday for me.

The Maltese must be the most religious people in the Christian world. I saw some of their devoutness on the fishing trip. We fished all morning to the north of Malta, catching some lampuki and baby tuna. Prayers before lunch and after. Trawling in the afternoon we caught more lampuki, which, I was told, were baby dolphin and made fine eating. Prayers were offered up for our safe return and then, with our fair-sized catch, we went ashore. Joe Vella drove me back to McGarth's flat. He told me some of the proud history of his people, and how they had, in the past, always managed in the end to eject anyone who tried to enslave them.

In 1947 the Maltese, with their fortitude during the great siege of the Second World War, recognized by the award of the George Cross to the island, were granted self-government, and at long last emerged as a small but very independent people, speaking their own language, which is a formidable mixture of Arabic and Italian.

McGarth was a keen sailor, and persuaded me to enter the *Nova Espero* for a handicap race organized by the Royal Malta Yacht Club, who on the same day were competing against some boats from Syracuse. A young naval officer volunteered to act as crew for me, and at the bang of a gun we were off. The *Nova* was well up against the leaders when I decided to hoist the spinnaker. I made a mess of the job; it filled all right—but unfortunately it was under water at the time. The *Nova* pulled up sharply and before I could sort things out we were down among the stragglers. The Club must have been generous with their handicapping, for to our amazement we got second prize. Sir Gerald Creasy, the Civil Governor of Malta, who was giving out the prizes, handed me a silver spoon on which was engraved the Club's flag. It is a souvenir I shall always treasure.

Captain John Illingworth, commodore of the Club, invited Mac and me to lunch and, later on, to a barbecue in honour of the visiting Italians. Something went wrong with the arrangements for the latter, for we never left the Navy boat taking us over to Gozo Islands, and we finished up eating fried sausages. I met the members of the Italian team, and was glad to see one or two I had come across in Syracuse.

There were so many interesting places to visit, and so many people to meet in Malta, that most of my recollections are kaleidoscopic with clear-cut pictures here and there. Musta Church is one of these. When I went there the sudden beauty of it caught me unawares. Pure snow-white walls panelled in royal blue and gold, a huge dome—the third largest in the world—and a riot of colourful pictures. I had never seen a church look so pure and sacred inside.

The ancient town of Notabile, one-time capital of Malta, seen in moonlight, is another unforgettable memory. One night, after dinner, Mac and I walked to the town, entered through the portcullis in the wall, and wandered about its narrow, dimly lit streets. There was hardly a soul about. Large buildings in yellow ochre stone, with windows guarded by ornamental ironwork, and strong embossed doors, lined the streets. It was quiet and sedate, like an old man sitting dreaming of the past. Instinctively talking in whispers we walked to an outer wall. Beyond the massive stonework was a sheer drop of a hundred feet or more. Away in the distance and far below us lay Valetta and Sliema, their twinkling lights matching the stars above.

One other scene I shall always remember is the sight of the walls standing high and strong round Valetta, bearing the name of a former Grand Master who ruled the people during the Turkish siege. Even the German and Italian bombs only put in a few dents and scars.

During the remainder of my visit I went several times with Joe Vella in his car for long runs around the island. Crumbling stone walls bounding the tiny fields, with usually a wind-driven water-pump in one corner; chapels and roadside shrines; Malta's one and only wood of straggly pines, planted by a former Grand Master as a place to hunt game (rabbits); all these fixed firmly in my mind a picture of the rural life of Malta, where even hard work brings only small returns.

The day before my proposed departure Mrs. Illingworth took me to see a polo match between the Navy and the Army. Here I was intro-duced to Lady Mountbatten, who, much to my embarrassment, made some very complimentary remarks to me. During the game I noticed she talked chiefly about the welfare of the men under her husband's

Stromboli and its wisp of volcanic smoke

Sicilian coastal craft with a cargo of sand

A lateen sailing coaster displaying an eye, St. George and the Dragon, and a mermaid blowing a trumpet

Catanian sculpture with rampant horses spurting water from their nostrils

Papier mache statues of the founders of Messina

74

command, and what could be done for their entertainment during off-duty hours. In the evening Joe Vella, together with all the friendly crew I had met in Sicily, and their wives, took me out to an hotel in the country for a farewell dinner. Here a long table set out under the stars had been arranged for us, with flowers and an imposing array of bottles. At the end of a succession of delicious courses, I got up and toasted the company, expressing my gratitude for their many kindnesses.

September 13th—my day of departure. Although I had been an extremely haphazard guest with Mac, he had been a very tolerant host, and had done everything in his power to make my stay interesting; always trying to put food inside me, for he insisted I was too thin. It was difficult to tell him how much I appreciated his hospitality, but I did my best.

Joe, the boatman for the R.M.Y.C., rowed me out to the *Nova*, sitting trim and graceful at her moorings with a new coat of copper paint on her under-water sections (bless the Navy). When I told Joe I was leaving that afternoon for Pantelleria, he looked up at the sky, solemnly shook his head and said, "Don't go today, there will be no wind by evening, and what there is now is blowing against you." Knowing that Joe had been a boatman there all his life I expected him to be right, and went ashore again to try to get some duty-free cigarettes. I was granted this privilege as a special concession, together with a Bill of Health for Pantelleria, an eloquent document which read:

CLEAN BILL OF HEALTH
CUSTOM HOUSE, MALTA

It is hereby certified, upon the departure from the Port of Valetta, in the Island of Malta, of the

1.	Name of $\begin{cases} \text{Steam} \\ \text{Motor} \\ \text{Sailing} \end{cases}$ Vessel	..	..		YACHT *Nova Espero*
2.	Flag ..	.. ..	.. ..	.. ..	BRITISH
3.	Name of Master	..	.. ..	.. ..	CHARLES VIOLET
4.	Tonnage ..	.. ..	.. ..	..	ONE
5.	Number of Crew (including Master)				ONE
6.	Number of Passengers	..	..	..	NIL
7.	Bound for	..	.. ..	.. ..	PANTELLERIA

that by the grace of God, good health is enjoyed throughout these possessions, without suspicion of Plague or any Contagious disease whatever.

In Faith whereof, this Clean Bill of Health is issued, under the Seal of this Department, this 12TH day of SEPTEMBER, One thousand nine hundred and 52.

COLLECTOR OF CUSTOMS.

E

Joe Maceirca (so many Josephs among the Maltese) was waiting for me on the quay when I returned from the customs. He and I had become very good friends since I had met him on Vella's boat in Messina. A Government official, and well known for his charity among the poor, he had been able to give me a picture of the struggle behind the scenes over Malta's claim for self-government. He must have realized that I was travelling on a very slim amount of money, for he had in his car for me a box of tinned foodstuffs, wine, and a large home-made cake.

Joe—the boatman—shook his head at me on the 14th. No sailing that day. On the morning of the 15th I got a nod, so I hurried ashore, filled my water-bottles, left a note of thanks at the Club, got some fresh loaves of bread, came back aboard, gave Joe something for his trouble and weather forecasting, hoisted all sail, and glided slowly out of Malta's secure harbour.

11

THE FORGOTTEN ISLAND

BOATMAN JOE was right about the weather, for once clear of the harbour I found a gentle south-easterly blowing. My course now being nearly due west I was able to hoist the spinnaker which, when brought under control, pushed the *Nova* along at three knots. The sombre hues of Malta, brightened by the fierce sunlight, passed slowly by on my left; then came the narrow channel separating the island of Gozo. Not having been there I altered course to pass close by, and saw a pretty little village and the foot of one of the steep, high slopes which form the island. Seeing some people bathing I ventured still further in, but when a bather stopped swimming a few yards from me and stood up with the water only waist high, I realized the shallowness of the water, and looking over the side I was shocked to see the sandy bottom was clearly visible. Curiosity, having nearly put me ashore, was banished from my mind, and the *Nova* headed for deeper water.

Cliffs rising hundreds of feet straight up from the sea dominated the western end of Gozo; their dark basalt sides glistened redly in the rays of the setting sun ahead. Before the twilight had disappeared from the sky Gozo was a hazy blob on the horizon.

Wind came with the darkness; the seas mounted high astern, and breaking crests began their sinister roar around me. Life ashore had softened me and I was filled with fear. Reefing down proved a wet and difficult business, for I could not see what I was doing, and there were no stars visible to lighten the surrounding blackness. I kept at the tiller all night and by morning I was sub-human, just a wet lump of humanity longing for nothing but warmth and oblivion. Taking down the reefed main I left the *Nova* to look after us and then, not caring in which direction we were heading, I went below and flung myself on the bunk. Sleep proved impossible, for the *Nova* was lurching violently in the seas, but I closed my burning eyes and soon regained enough energy to get up and make some tea, after which I did not feel too bad apart from an ache in my eyes.

September 16th was a poor day with a strong wind and continuing large broken seas. My principal anxiety was the non-appearance of Pantelleria. I had hoped to sight its tall peak by evening, but when the sun set I was still fruitlessly scanning the horizon on each point of the compass.

Another bad night followed, for the wind increased in strength and at 2 a.m. I had to lower the reefed mainsail and continue under jib and mizen. "Damn it," I thought. "It looks as though I shall have a gale to contend with, and that will probably put Pantelleria behind me; and who wants to beat about in this mess?" Visibility was at a minimum during the night and it wasn't much better when daylight came, for cotton-wool clouds hung low over the sea. However, I had one piece of luck which bucked up my spirits. Just before 10 a.m. the clouds thinned and I could faintly make out a watery sun; dashing below I grabbed my sextant and took a hurried sight, from which I worked out my longitude. It coincided with that of Pantelleria, so now I knew the island lay either due south or due north. That useful but now little valued oddity, instinct, told me it was north, so in that direction I went. Within an hour the vague outline of a mountain was to be seen, and my lost island was found. My eyes were very painful now and I looked forward to at least twelve hours' deep sleep.

At midday houses were clearly visible, with the usual terracing climbing like ladders up the steep mountainside. The highest part of the island was veiled in cloud, and below the coastline looked very forbidding, edged with black volcanic rock over which the heavy seas broke in a smother of white. No sandy beaches, no coves for shelter. For the first time in the Mediterranean I did not have to worry about my course, for at Malta I had obtained numerous large-scale Admiralty charts; they were given me free of charge for they were stamped "Cancelled." With the confidence born of knowledge I swept along the south coast towards the western tip and the port of Pantelleria. My chart showed that the port had two harbours; one with six feet of water alongside the quay and shallow elsewhere, the other with deep water but apparently no place to dock alongside. I decided to enter the

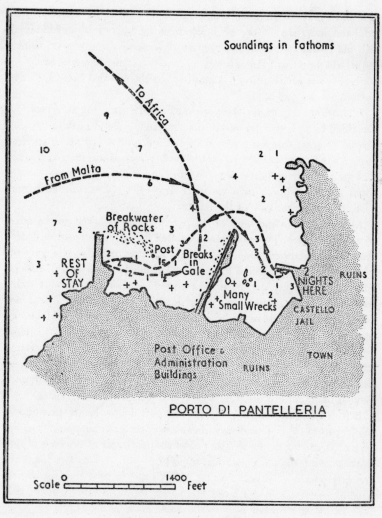

The port of PANTELLERIA

first and tie up to the quay. The wind, now coming off the land, was fitful and uncertain. Discretion being the better part of valour I lowered sail, put on the outboard, and very slowly entered the tiny port, thinking all the time that I did not want a repetition of my two groundings in Sicily. My need for caution was increased by the fact that I could see the bottom all the way in.

A small sailing coaster took up much of the space on the quay, so I decided to go higher up nearer the town, but a burst of shouting and waving of arms stopped me, and I switched off the engine. A sudden gust of wind came and before I could get organized I was mixed up with a cluster of rowing boats. Many willing and excited hands caught the ropes I threw ashore; then we were dragged ignominiously from our nest of boats to the side of the coaster.

All the children and most of the populace had gathered on the quay to watch me dock. Three policemen pushed through the crowd, boarded the coaster, brushed aside the skipper and crew who were trying to talk to me, and demanded my papers. I handed over a wad of papers which included my driving-licence and the important Bill of Health from Malta. One copied down some details in his notebook, one stood on deck with his carbine, and the third went below and opened lockers, looking, I suppose, for contraband. When all was completed to their satisfaction my papers were handed back with the exception of my passport, which they were going to take to police headquarters. Then they relaxed and became human, so I sat them round the cockpit and handed them cups of tea, very sweet to suit Mediterranean tastes.

Before I was allowed to go ashore the port doctor had to pronounce me free from contagious disease. In about a quarter of an hour's time he arrived, sweating profusely. He poked a damp finger at the base of my neck, pronounced me a well man and off he went, shaking two hundred and fifty pounds of superfluous fat which I should have thought would have melted away in the heat. The police followed shortly after, and then the coaster moved away to the outer harbour. I moored the *Nova* to my satisfaction; bow made fast a few inches from the quay and anchor out from the stern.

Pantalleria looked a sad, poor little town. The advancing Allied wave had swept over it, smashed it, and carried on northwards, leaving the smoking ruins behind, forgotten. They are still there today, a mute reminder of the tides of war, the islanders being too poor to do much except sweep up the dust.

That first evening on the island I walked along the quay with my escort of chattering boys, and stopped in front of the one solid building among the ruins. It was a square fort built of black stone and used, I learned later, for housing political prisoners. A man came up to me, took my arm, and led me to a canvas-covered stall on which were piles of grapes. He picked out a bunch, went to a nearby tap and washed them carefully, and then presented them to me. When I offered him some money he became indignant—they were a gift. Not content with that he took me to a café and insisted on buying me a coffee.

Early to bed that night and I got in fourteen hours' continuous sleep. The pain in my eyes had disappeared the next morning, when I was awakened by the cigarette chorus. My grape-buying friend arrived at 7 a.m.; I gave him some tea and a packet of cigarettes, and when I had finished breakfast he took me for a ride on his motor-bike. As we bumped over the stony roads, past tiny farmhouses, I thought of what a British farmer would say if expected to farm there. I am sure he would have dismissed the bulk of each farm as a cinder heap and the patches of terracing as marginal land.

The countryside looked desolate on my side of the island. Stunted trees grew on the higher slopes of the mountain, still shrouded in cloud. The grass was coarse and wild flowers were absent. No wonder the majority of the people looked poverty-stricken and apathetic.

Upon returning to the town I took my new friend for a drink and bought a bottle of wine to take back to the boat. It cost the equivalent of one shilling! Made from raisin grapes it had the same delicious flavour as that I had sampled in Syracuse. In the afternoon I went to the black fort, which also housed the police, to see what had happened to my passport. There were no guards about from whom to enquire the whereabouts of the police office, so I quietly searched on my own. Climbing some stone steps I reached a row of mediaeval looking cells, some occupied by pallid prisoners, either gazing through a window or lying on their bed-boards. Turning up a corridor to my right I saw a guard sitting in an alcove cut into the stone. When I approached to enquire the way he exploded into a torrent of Italian. I managed to get in a few "Stampa passport" as he led me away to the office, where a wordy battle was waged ending in my having my passport stamped and returned to me.

On 19th September a messenger arrived before breakfast telling me to go and see the port captain right away. I told him I would come when I had had breakfast. Half way through the meal he was there again bidding me come at once, but I remained adamant—after breakfast and not before. When I had eventually finished I went on deck and found the port captain himself waiting patiently on the quay. All he wanted to tell me was that he had received warning of strong winds from the west, which would make the port unsafe for my boat; he then turned and introduced two men who were staring at the *Nova*. One bore a remarkable resemblance to Herbert Marshall, the film actor, and was the owner of a fish factory (a thousand employed before the war, now thirty). I remember nothing about the other except that he spoke a little English. Taking all three on board I motored out of the harbour and, carefully following the directions of "Herbert Marshall," entered the other larger port. Once there the port captain exercised his authority, and ordered a couple of coasters to move so that I could tie up to a few square yards of concrete, where all the boats loaded and unloaded their cargoes. Not wishing to be a nuisance to the ships, I insisted on berthing in a corner where I could jump from the boat on to a rock.

There were several trading schooners in the port which were from fifty to seventy feet long. They made a brave show with their graceful clipper bows, gay colours, and tawny sails. The only concession to modern times had been the installation of a diesel auxiliary. These ships had arrived to take away Pantelleria's raisin crop; that and firewood are the only two exports from the island. A sailor from one of the traders rowed up to me and, in perfect English, invited me to come and look over his ship. He had been a prisoner-of-war in England until 1947, and had not minded much, but the subject of the weather drew groans from him as he recalled life on an English farm in winter. The lack of freeboard on his heavily laden boat amazed me, for the water was deck level amidships, and only two or three feet below the gunwales fore and aft. "Good heavens," I exclaimed, "you don't mean to tell me it's safe to make a voyage with the ship practically sunk." He laughed, pointed to the *Nova*, and said, "I would not cross the harbour in a boat as small as that.'' Clambering over the boxes of raisins that filled the holds and overflowed on to the deck, I was shown the crew's sleeping quarters. They were small and dark, with only sitting head-room. I was told that the crew usually slept on deck, and was not surprised. Cooking was also done on deck over a charcoal fire.

Next to me was an old boat fitted with a derrick. On Saturday, 20th September, the owner, a Sicilian, came uninvited aboard the *Nova* in the morning. I gave him tea and a cigarette, and learned that he had collected a crew and a diver in Sicily, and was now engaged in recovering scrap metal from the many small vessels sunk around the island during the war. He invited me to go with them and take some photographs. I accepted with alacrity, and soon the old tub chugged her way out of the harbour and into the heavy swell outside; she wallowed horribly, making water stream across her deck. Her carefree crew laughed at me as I scampered on to the hatch.

We followed the coast for a mile or so, and in the meantime the skipper and some of the crew festooned the rigging with salt fish to dry in the sun. We moored to two buoys marking a wreck, brought the boat round to meet the seas, and then the diver slowly attired himself in his underwater suit with the aid of a boy assistant. At each stage of the proceedings I was asked to take a photograph. I photographed him being lowered into the water; I photographed everything and everybody in sight. I had to—they insisted. The diver went down forty feet; I could still see his shadowy form with the bubbles from his helmet making a bright greenish stream against the dark blue of the water. Explosives, handled with supreme carelessness, were lowered to him, and he placed them on the wreck. The boat was moved away a few hundred yards and then a man in a skiff detonated the bombs. A heavy, dull thud, a cascade of water shot into the air, and then a mad scramble by the man in the skiff to pick up stunned fish that floated up to the surface.

A black cloud rising above the horizon made the skipper call it a day, and we started back. On the way back it began to rain, so the diver and I took shelter in the engine-room, where a two-cylinder twenty-four horse-power diesel thumped away. Looking round the narrow space I saw what an old basket I was in. Water weeped along every seam between the black, ancient planks. When we finally made port they insisted on my having the midday meal with them. Nothing loth, I was led to the most bombed part of the town, and finally we stopped outside a door at the end of a very narrow passageway. Inside was a cellar, probably all that remained of a large house or church, with a dark, mouldering, arched ceiling, and a tiny window high up, unglazed and protected by a heavy iron grille. There were camp beds, a table, two benches, many barrels, boxes of explosives with their contents spilling on to the floor, a heap of rotting potatoes and a dozen wooden boxes of raisins. I sampled some of the latter—they were very good eating.

Nectar-like wine was thrust in large quantities upon me, and under its influence the cellar became a pleasant looking room with rose-washed walls. The skipper, having taken all his salt fish from the boat, now carefully hung them round the walls of the cellar. From a small alcohol stove a very savoury smell arose. The Italians certainly can make food smell tempting, and even the most jaded appetite is stirred. The rain stopped, and the skipper took down the fish and hung them up again outside from some ropes in the alley. The meal, when finally ready, consisted of spaghetti over which was ladled a sauce of chopped meat, tomatoes, onions, garlic, raisins and potatoes. I enjoyed it very much, but I had to ask them to remove a part of my helping before I started, explaining that the English were no longer used to such mountains of food. The next course was baby fish fried in olive oil, but I could not manage any more, and so nibbled a few grapes to keep them happy. A prodigious amount of wine was being consumed all the time, and things were becoming lively. Up to now the conversation had been chiefly carried on by signs, aided by my few words of Italian. Suddenly memories of schoolboy Latin floated to the surface of my vinous mind. "*Mensa*," I shouted, slapping the table. Their open-mouthed astonishment changed to roars of laughter as I trotted out further Latin phrases.

It was dark by the time I returned to the *Nova*—we had enjoyed quite a long lunch.

The long awaited gale blew that day, and I had great difficulty in preventing the *Nova* from bumping against the nearby rock. The ex-prisoner-of-war asked me whether my boat would survive in waves like those in the stormy weather outside. It was hard to convince him that the *Nova* would stand a better chance than his overloaded craft.

September 23rd was my birthday, and strangely enough I was given several presents, although no one knew about the date. One sailor handed me about four pounds of raisins, while the ex-prisoner gave me some figs dried by his mother and beautifully parcelled up in bay-leaves. Another man filled up my water-bottle without being asked, and finally I was invited on board the old coaster for a meal. She stank so much that I asked whether they would mind my eating up on deck, making the feeble excuse that I liked sitting in the sun.

I had hoped to sail the following day but the wind was dead against me for Cape Bon, my next objective. This famous cape is the eastern horn of the great Bay of Tunis, and I was looking forward to visiting a fringe of the Dark Continent.

12

NORTH AFRICA

My old friend the south-east wind was waiting for me once the breaking-up influence of Pantelleria mountain was passed.

Before I had left, the skipper of the old salvage vessel had come aboard and hung up a large bunch of his rather smelly salt fish. I suspect that he felt a ship was not complete without a supply of these swinging in the sun. I did not have the heart to throw it overboard, and I promised myself that I would give it to the first hungry looking Arab I saw.

When about ten miles out a tiny humming-bird made several attempts to land on the boat, but the *Nova* was swinging about rather violently and the would-be passenger could not make it. When its vivid colours were last sighted it was trying to head for the island. I saw many fish breaking surface in this part of the sea; I must have been passing through a large shoal on its way to new feeding-grounds. The fishermen from the island could have reaped a good harvest if they had been able to afford powered craft.

It was a tremendous thrill when in the afternoon I sighted the dark hills of Africa; before nightfall Cape Bon was clearly seen ahead, but it was dark before I actually rounded its rocky point. The wind got up in fierce gusts, and pushed the *Nova* over on to her beam ends. Getting the mainsail down, I let her go more easily under jib and mizen. On my starboard bow was the dim outline of Zembra island, which rises straight up from the sea to 1,421 feet, so not wishing to get in its lee, I hoisted the mainsail, reefed and drove the boat hard to clear the weather side. It was touch and go for a while, but we got by with only a few yards to spare. The importance of large-scale charts, and the advantages of possessing them, were most apparent in this case, for although it was night I knew that there was clear, deep water right up to the side of Zembra. During the rest of the night I sailed around the Bay of Tunis, and when it was light enough to see the shore I hove-to and got some sleep.

Coming on deck and blinking in the strong sunlight a couple of hours later, I noticed that the wind had changed, and that the *Nova* had altered her course with it and was now near the shore. As soon as I corrected her desire for landing I had time to gaze at the magnificent panorama of this huge bay: in the distance the high hills that formed Cape Bon, then the low land round the centre, rising to the high ground of the western point called Cape Farina.

I had been advised to make for Bizerta, which lies about twenty miles west of Farina. Unfortunately the wind blew from the west and made a nasty steep sea now that it met the swell caused by yesterday's south-easterly. For hours I tacked towards the western cape and made little progress. When I finally came parallel to a diminutive island, on which stood a lighthouse, I must have got in an easterly current, for there I stuck, each tack bringing me back to the same place opposite the lighthouse. I later met a man in Bizerta who had been doing some repair work to the light; he told me that he and one of the keepers had spent most of their time watching my fight against wind, seas, and current, wondering what I would do, and getting quite worried.

I saw that conditions were hopeless for continuing that day, so I upped with the helm, and sailed into the lee of Cape Farina. Here it was smooth and placid with the sea a bright pea-green; a sandy cove, backed by green scrub and prickly pears, lay directly ahead. Halfway up the hill above the cove was a small mosque surrounded by a collection of miserable huts. Not long after I had anchored a gang of Arab urchins came swarming down from the huts, and stood on the shore shouting to me. From their beckoning waves I gathered they wanted me to go ashore—not me.

Towards evening the wind died away, and not wishing to remain at anchor in the cove all night with that colony of ruffians so near, I put on the outboard and set off once more for Bizerta. But it was hopeless, the waves were still too big for the *Nova* to push against them bow on. Back I came again, deciding that I might as well risk staying the night. The boys, now accompanied by some men, greeted my return with howls of delight, which I did not share. This time I anchored a bit further out, and went into the cabin to get a meal, after which I went through my customary routine of tapping the aneroid barometer. It fell a tenth, and I guessed, rightly for once, that another change of wind would be coming soon.

At 12.15 I heard a halliard tap against the mast, and went on deck to find the boat now facing south, from which came a faint, warm, dry air, heavily laden with a hundred different odours, muskiness predominating.

Third time lucky. During the night I sailed between the high escarpment of Africa and some small islands, the wind sometimes strong and sometimes weak.

During the long hours at the helm in the moonless night, I would forget time and place and sink into a deep reverie. In my imagination the *Nova Espero* would become a Phoenician galley, and instead of facing the trials of single-handed sailing I would picture myself as a pilot of two thousand years ago, with the responsibility for the safe arrival of crew, captain, and cargo. No escapist dreams of trouble-free passages on these occasions! Instead the threat of sudden total shipwreck if my navigation proved faulty oppressed my mind, though no lack of self-confidence was allowed to show on my face. Then the long-sought landfall would come into sight, the worry verging on panic would be swept away in a flood of relief, and my mythical galley, under the guidance of its still impassive pilot, would change course towards the anchorage. I am always a hero in my dreams!

At 3 o'clock in the morning I was off Cape Zebil, and by the grace of God, missed by inches a partly submerged wreck. I only noticed it by the phosphorescent gleam of the seas breaking over its jagged edges, and it was not shown on the Admiralty chart I had of this area. Once in the Bay of Bizerta I backed the jib to windward so that the boat would only drift slowly towards the other shore, then when she was nearly there I merely turned her round and headed in the opposite direction. These manoeuvres gave me an hour of freedom from the tiller, and enabled me to wash, shave, and have a meal.

During one of these slow tacks across the bay I was amused by an incident that I watched from a cabin porthole. An Arab fishing-boat returning from a night's work passed by, then, seeing what they thought to be a deserted boat, turned back, and made a circle round me.

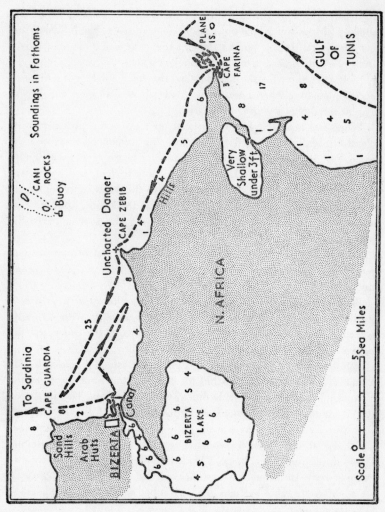

NORTH
AFRICA

89

Some shouting took place, and then a man picked up a coil of rope and took up his position in the bow, ready to make fast to the *Nova* and tow her into port. At this point I thought the game had gone far enough, and poked my head out of the hatch.

I felt a bit sorry for the man holding the rope, for he got a burst of derisive laughter when I was seen. Evidently he had been the one to egg on the others to salvage the *Nova*.

When the boat and I were spruced up I eased the jib over to its correct side and we began to beat into the harbour. I regretted the hanging about so long outside, for the wind began to blow a regular harmattan from the land. I did not have time to reef, and had a very difficult half-hour before I anchored close to the sandy shore inside the harbour. Although only a hundred yards away from land, I put out two anchors which dragged a little before they dug deep enough into the bottom.

The sleep I tried to get was broken by the arrival of customs and police in a motor launch. When they left, my wine was finished and my cigarettes nearly so.

Bizerta has been rebuilt since the war. From where I lay at anchor it looked a beautiful city of modern white buildings, with windows screened by jalousie blinds of every hue. Between the shore and the houses was a long avenue of royal palms.

While wondering how on earth I could get ashore I was hailed by a man in a row-boat. He invited me to bring the *Nova* across to the Yacht Club and moor alongside one of their boat floats. This invitation solved my immediate problem, so I hoisted sail and followed my host.

A crowd gathered to look at the little boat from England. They were a new type to me—French colonials. Very free and easy and hospitable. I invited the young Frenchman, Claude de Solleu, who had hailed me, to come aboard. He brought his mother and father with him, and we all sat down in the cabin to drink tea. It was hot below, and Claude asked if he might take off his coat. "Of course," I replied, "go ahead." When he did so I was surprised to see that he wore a shoulder holster, something I thought only Chicago gangsters carried. "Why do you wear such a thing?" I asked. "Is it dangerous ashore?" "Not in the day-time," he replied, "but it certainly is at night, especially if you go anywhere near the Arab quarter." He then explained to me that the

The forbidding landscape of Western Sardinia

Part of ancient Bonifacio's walled town overhanging the sea

Keepers of the peace in Pantelleria

The Governor of Malta presents the Author with a Maltese silver spoon

(Photo : Times of M...

92

riots which were causing so much trouble in Tunisia at that time were mainly the paid work of underground communists who did not really give two hoots for the welfare of the Arabs, but only wished to bring trouble on the French Government. Later on an Arab gave me a different picture of the troubles and their causes.

Claude, who spoke fairly good English, having been attached to the British Navy during the war, told me that his father had been awarded the M.B.E. for his assistance to the Allies at the time of the North African campaigns. He was a pilot, now retired, for Bizerta.

The next day was a restful one. I watched the French youth of the Club race some hard-chine boats, somewhat similar to the Snipe class we have in England, and drank wine in the club-house. On 29th September Claude took me to the open-air market so that I could get some cheap provisions. These African markets have remained unchanged through the centuries. Among the smells and cries of the vendors I rubbed shoulders with disreputable beggars, smart, vivacious French-women, and veiled Arab women. (Why is black *de rigeur* for all the poorer classes of Arab women at the eastern end of the Mediterranean, while towards the west white and cream are the only permissible colours?)

The French, may they be forgiven, are shortly going to prohibit the sale of fruit, meat and fish from this collection of colourful stalls, and house a selected few in a modern, partly closed-in building. More hygienic, perhaps, but asking for trouble, and at the same time causing the loss of an interesting survival from an older Africa.

I went to the cinema in the evening with the de Solleu family. There were two main films—one was about life in a nudist camp; very revealing, and covered me with embarrassment. It certainly would not have passed the British censorship. The other was an excellent picture of a gang of delinquents in Mexico, produced, directed and filmed in that country.

I had hoped to leave the following day, but there was no wind, only fickle puffs coming from all points of the compass. Disregarding Claude's warning about trying to photograph Arab women, I set off to attempt to do so without their being aware of the fact. Walking down the streets with my camera swinging in my hand, I snapped many veiled women in their cream coloured voluminous drapes and black yashmaks.

F

When I saw a subject coming I would walk towards her with the camera pressed against my thigh, and then, humming to hide the click, I'd take a random shot. The results were awful, being chiefly of road or sky, although one or two just managed to be recognizable.

On my way back I passed the pilot station. Two Arab sailors were sitting in front. One, tall, black-haired and swarthy, called out to me in English as I went by, "Come, we wish to speak with you, Englishman." Wondering what it was all about I sauntered over. The tall Arab turned to the other, a bulbous man with a drooping moustache, and said something. It must have been a request for another chair and wine, for the fat man came back with both. The bottle circled once or twice and I declared it good wine. Cigarettes followed. When we were puffing contentedly the tall lean one began a tirade against the French. I wrote down later in my log book what he said to me, for it showed how two working Arabs, and possibly many more, were thinking. He started, "We like the English, they promised independence to the Indians, and gave it to them. My countrymen will honour any people who keep their word. Now the French, who have always been poor colonists, are deceivers. One cannot trust them, they use my country and my people to their own advantage. We want our independence as much as you would if your country were ruled by the Germans." He then continued, "Your mother took nine months to produce you; so did mine. I have a wife and three children; their needs are the same as anyone else's, but a Frenchman doing the same amount of work a month as me gets ninety thousand francs; I get seventeen thousand." He finished up by saying, "We don't like the Egyptians; they are not real Arabs, and only make trouble for trouble's sake, but you do think, don't you, that we Arabs have a right to independence." "Why yes, indeed," I replied, for I was not going to start an argument on the relative needs of man; he looked too fierce! I shook them both by the hand and thanked them for an interesting afternoon. As I walked away he called out, "Let the people in England know how we feel."

Back on the boat I decided to clean the plug and carburettor on the outboard. My work was very much handicapped by a little girl we called Mosquito, a brown little creature always running about with bare feet. She was the daughter of Auguste, the Club boatman and caretaker. His family had been in Africa for generations, and now looked Arabic.

Mosquito had developed a passion for my malted-milk tablets, which I used at sea when cooking was not possible. She would beg a couple, run away, and be back again a few moments later asking for more. When I finally left I had none.

On 1st October there was wind, but dead against me for my next stopping-place—Sardinia. A French dentist and his wife called on me, and said that they had come to take me for a motor drive so that I could see more of the country before I left. It was impossible to go more than five miles outside the town without a permit, but none the less it proved an interesting run past large sandy hills, innumerable French forts and depots. When we passed through an Arab village I remembered my conversation of the previous day. The huts were either built of mud and straw, or odds and ends of packing-cases covered with rusty corrugated iron sheets. I could see no windows or means of ventilation. Goats and chickens wandered in and out of these squalid places, and I could well imagine the smell inside.

Turning to the dentist, Charles Luippi, I asked, "Have they always lived in such conditions?" "Oh yes," he replied. "They are quite happy and content there."

Some of the valleys were extensively cultivated, and the soil looked dark and rich, but the oxen still slowly toiled among the ridges—no tractors. I had dinner with Charles and his wife and afterwards played Canasta. It was all very serious, but having to count up the points in French was fun for me.

There was a very bad storm during the night, and the heavy rain played a devil's tattoo on the thin, resounding plywood above my head. Lightning and thunder flashed and crashed over the town, and it did not stop until daybreak. When I got up I saw that there was water in the cockpit up to the seat. I was not surprised when Auguste told me that four inches of rain had fallen in the night.

I did some very necessary bo'sun's work during the morning, for I had postponed my sailing again because the wind was still unfavourable. In the afternoon I went sailing around the harbour in an Ace class boat, very fast but very wet.

I had wanted to eat in an Arab restaurant before leaving Africa, and when Charles Luippi heard that I had not departed he called for me in the evening and took me off to one, visiting several places on the way for aperitifs. A plate of highly spiced chopped goat's meat, surrounded by a wall of grey looking rice, was placed in front of me, and then some sauce, red-hot, was poured on top. Once that mound of rather rancid mess was inside me I imagined I had enjoyed it and said so. It took several glasses of strong red wine to alleviate the burning taste it left behind. My host said, "Well, that's *cous-cous*, now you must have a brick." Although my stomach felt completely full I thought a brick, whatever it might be, would be a good thing to have on top to hold things in place. "Right," I said, "nothing venture, nothing do." The brick, when it arrived, consisted of a complete egg, surrounded by some chopped green peppers, all inside a lump of glass-like batter. I finished it, and gulped down a glass of white wine.

At 5 a.m. I awoke feeling sick; at 6 a.m. I was, and continued to be for the rest of the day. By the time evening arrived I thought I was going to die. In Bermuda I once had dysentery; and on this occasion a form of it returned. Because I had not put my head above deck no one came to visit me. "Blast these polite Frenchmen," I thought. "Here I am dying and can't get anyone to fetch some help." A band of pain above my eyes felt as though I'd crushed my head, but I swallowed four aspirins and then felt slightly better.

For two long days I lay on my bunk, a very miserable aching person, but on the morning of the 5th of October I came up on deck to view the outside world, and saw that the wind was blowing off the land. A favourable breeze—too good to miss. I lugged my large water-bottles ashore (I had taken nothing but water since that fatal Arabic food), filled them up at the Club's tap, and then found Auguste. "Where have you been?" he said. "I thought you were sleeping ashore." Then he looked closely at my unshaven face and added, "You look very pale, have you been ill?" When I told him what had happened he laughed and said, "You should stick to European food, or at least have it cooked at home, never from an Arab restaurant."

Just behind Bizerta is a large salt-water lake, connected to the harbour by a narrow dredged channel. Even the small (about one foot) tide in the Mediterranean causes a very strong current going in and out. It was rushing in when I left, and with only a light breeze blowing I had a difficult job getting out, at one time being nearly pushed on the corner of the breakwater.

13

BLINDNESS

GLANCING AT my chronometer as soon as I cleared the harbour, I noticed that the time was 9.15 a.m. Within thirty-six hours I hoped to be anchored in a snug cove on the south-east tip of Sardinia, 130 miles to the north. The fair wind petered out by mid-morning, and I thought we were in for a journey of several days, just drifting with odd winds to the north.

My morale was low after two days of fasting and sickness, and I wished I had stayed a day or two longer in Bizerta to recover my *joie de vivre*. I was down below in the cabin, drinking tea and munching dry biscuits when the first puff of wind arrived. It came from the north-west, and by hauling in the mainsheet as tight as possible I could just hold my course. This cool wind plus the fact that a quicker journey was now probable revived my flagging spirits.

There was a glorious sunset in a cloudless sky that night. Land had disappeared, and it seemed a special display for a minute speck in the vastness of sky and water. As soon as the fiery sun dipped below the horizon the western sky turned peach-coloured, then orange, and finally a deep rich red. At the same time the sky changed from duck-egg blue to indigo velvet as night came stealing across from the east. The glow in the west faded like red-hot iron cooling. It was all over by 7 o'clock, a warning that long nights were ahead.

The wind freshened, and the *Nova* thrust her shoulders hard into the oncoming waves, throwing spray over herself with abandonment. Sitting in the cockpit as we raced through the night one of Stanley Smith Senior's jingles kept recurring in my mind. Every time I coughed he would say, "Ah, Charles, it isn't the cough that carries you off, it's the coffin they carry you off in."

At midnight I had a bad scare, for though the force of the wind remained unaltered, we entered a patch of pyramid seas which broke all over the *Nova*, filling the cockpit and, as the hatch was open, putting a foot of water in the cabin. I immediately lowered the mainsail and closed the hatch. The boat was unmanageable, plunging and lurching about like an unbroken horse. I just clutched the cockpit coaming with one hand and bailed like fury with the other. Quite suddenly it was all over, and the *Nova* was riding up and down over more rhythmic waves. While getting the water out of the cabin, as the *Nova* jogged along quietly under jib and mizen, I realized the possible reason for that nasty patch of sea. Getting out the chart I looked carefully along the track course and spotted a dotted line encircling a small area of water 240 feet deep, but immediately around it the sea-bottom was nearly 6,000 feet down. It must have been that undersea hill that caused all the commotion.

Now satisfied that I had not sailed among some reefs, I hoisted the mainsail and continued on my way. Two hours later I had to reef it, for the wind increased. At 3 a.m. I shook it out again, then tied a reef in once more at 5 a.m. The wind eased at 9 a.m., and with fingers now sore with all the tying and untying of wet reef-points, I had the whole mainsail up again, hoping the fickle wind had finally made up her mind.

I felt desperately tired, and the old dysentery trouble was continuing, but a sight of Sardinia's jagged peaks at 10 o'clock gave me a little zest. All the rest of the day I plugged towards them over the rough seas. From misty blue to black, and from black to green and brown, they rose higher and higher above the horizon.

As the sun began to set, the mountains lost their individuality in shade, and became a featureless mass. I was able to tell that I was a little east of my course, and the wind, which fortunately had backed a little, now enabled me to make west of north, straight into the sun. Trying to make out a cove, plainly marked on the chart, I became acutely conscious of the brilliance of the setting sun. I endeavoured to shield my reluctant eyes from the glare, and vainly tried to see something resembling a place to anchor. The silhouetted mountains now looked the blackest and most vicious I had ever seen. They seemed to almost tear at the sky, as jagged, stark and wild as some imagined lunar landscape.

Soon I became aware of a deep booming sound, or rather sensation. The actual noise was not there, it was more an impression of immense power in the air. The throbbing pain increased above my eyes, which now felt as if they were lined with sand from the Sahara, sharp and grinding each time I blinked into the sun. My mouth became parched and dry, and my stomach heaved. I longed to be safely at anchor in the elusive cove hidden among the anonyminity of the rocky cliffs.

Cursing the sun boring into my eyes, and reviling my miserable body, I continued to peer ahead. Suddenly, to my horror, the black mountains climbed rapidly into the sky, blotting out all light as they did so. I clenched my fists and screwed them into my eye-sockets; when I took them away I tried desperately to see something, anything, but could not. I was blind! The terrible sickening truth of this came to me when I turned towards where the mast should be—there was nothing to see! I let out what must have been a heart-rending wail, barked my shin from knee to ankle as I scrambled out of the cockpit on to the cabin roof, and caught a sharp blow across the face from what was probably the weather backstay. I found the mainmast and then, in a crazy fit, tried to catch the jib to stop it flogging, overbalanced and fell flat on the foredeck; my feet caught in the jib-sheets and the next moment a lurch of the boat rolled me into the water. I suppose by this time I had become quite panic-stricken. I simply do not recollect getting on board again—the next thing I can remember is being once more in the cabin, sitting on the bunk with my head between my knees, groaning with the agony above my eyes.

I have read many descriptions of people getting into an hysterical state, and always thought their behaviour exaggerated and preposterous; I know now that the imaginative writer is not so inaccurate after all. The sudden horror of what had happened, this total blindness coming upon me so close to such a forbidding shore, had completely unnerved me. I could not think as I sat there, and so did not know where the boat was heading. Dimly and miserably I became aware that the next and final trouble might be upon me at any moment, a shock as we struck the rocks under the cliffs. I tried to listen for sound of breakers, but could only hear the roaring in my head. This extra terror was evidently too much for me, and I must have fainted. Nature now took a hand, for while I was unconscious the trouble with my eyes was partly cured. When I opened my eyes some time later I could see the shadowy outline of the cabin. I staggered into the fresh air, filled with relief and hope. The sun had long set, but there was a faint glimmer of twilight in the sky. My head still ached furiously, but it was wonderful to see the dark mass of land less than half a mile away. The *Nova*, bless her, had sailed very little towards the shore, probably coming up into the wind most of the time. I got her moving again, and when closer in I saw, as I rounded a rocky pinnacle about two hundred yards off-shore, a lovely semi-circle of lighter shade which could only be the sandy shore of the cove. The heaving water slowed to placidity as we carefully entered the sheltering arms of this cosy dent in the land. As quickly as my weariness would allow I lowered the sails and dropped anchor. A flood of relief swept over me, for lifting up my hands I could see their outline clearly, and over there the land enfolded in the night, and a joyful glimpse of twinkling lights high up the mountainside. An off-shore breeze brought the scent of wood smoke. All was peacefully quiet and utterly restful. The murmur of the swell on the rocks outside was no longer something to be feared, but a soft bass note from the sea-symphony.

With four aspirins to ease my violent headache I lay down on my bunk and was soon fast asleep.

14

SARDINIA

THE SUN shining through the portholes woke me up on my first morning in Sardinia. I stretched myself luxuriously on the bunk, indulged in a huge yawn, and thought of food. Twelve hours' sleep had worked wonders for me. By twisting round to reach the stove I contrived a breakfast-in-bed.

Curious as to my surroundings, I got up after breakfast and came on deck to see what my anchorage looked like in the broad light of day. It was beautiful in colour and shape. The shallow blue-green water was bounded by a perfect crescent of golden sand, with a small stream coming down from the foothills, which were covered in dark green scrub. The only signs of life were two cottages halfway up one of the hills, with blue smoke rising from the chimneys. On the southern of the rocky arms of the cove was the ruin of an ancient watch-tower. To the north I could see the coast fading into the distance, with several islands just off the shore. The background was always the dark magenta mountains. It would have suited me perfectly to have stayed there for a week or so, but "home for Christmas" was now my watchword.

During the remainder of that day I only covered twenty miles up the eastern side of Sardinia. The off-shore wind was fitful and vexing, but the wildness and ruggedness of the slowly unfolding scenery made my slow progress a pleasure. I had listened to the B.B.C. overseas broadcast that morning, and among the news items was an account of Sardinian bandits holding up several busloads of people and taking all their valuables, followed by the news that many police were now on the search both on land and sea. This information added piquancy to my close observation of all around me.

Making for a place grandiloquently called Port Corallo, an insignificant dent in the shore-line, I was surprised when I actually arrived there, for only one single-storey house could be seen, and the *Nova* had to anchor on a short line to stop her swinging on to the rocks on either side. Ahead of me was one small fishing boat, whose crew waved to me and, raising their arms in a drinking motion, invited me over. Unfortunately my head still ached, in spite of wearing sun-glasses, and the dysentery had returned, so I had to content myself with thanking them while, by cupping my hands together and resting my head against them, I hoped to convey the idea that I wished to sleep. When I closed my eyes my fugitive thoughts kept recalling the sights I had seen during the day. The line of fortified watch-towers which stood on every projecting point along the coast intrigued me. I suppose the Sardinian kings' main preoccupation in the past was with the ever-present threat of invasion. What with that, and the problem of coping with their own bloody-minded subjects, life must have been a turbulent affair.

There was not much sleep that night for me, because of having to get up so many times. I was glad when daylight arrived, though I did not like the increasing gusts of wind coming off the land. The fishing-boat returned with its big arc-lights on her stern still burning. The man at the tiller shouted to me as they passed, "Big wind coming today, stay close to the shore," and swept his hand up and down to illustrate the wind coming down the mountains. The man was absolutely right, for I had never experienced such a force of wind as came in mighty gusts from the Sardinian mountains. Even with only the jib and mizen the *Nova* was pushed over on to her side. Although no big waves bothered me, as I was close inshore, some of the stronger twisting gusts whipped off the surface of the water and threw it at me with such force that it felt like tiny pebbles. Fearing that my sails would blow out, I lowered them while under the lee of a cliff, then putting on the outboard I slowly puttered on, weaving my way through the rocks lining the shore. At the same time I continued my struggle with dysentery. When I emerged from the shelter of the cliffs the wind had another little joke waiting for me. A sudden blast came, so that the *Nova* heeled in response even though she was under bare poles, then it blew the jib up its stay, loosened the roughly-tied mizen, and had us over until the ports were submerged. When it had roared its way past us and out to sea I tied both sails firmly down. "Now, damn you, try that again," I shouted at the invisible but powerful enemy. The gale lessened in the afternoon and I was able to set sail again.

The impressive scenery continued, mountain after mountain, hill after hill, the land sometimes ending abruptly in high cliffs, and sometimes in low marshy patches edged with sand.

Cape Bellavista was a welcome sight, because just beyond lay a proper man-sized harbour. The lighthouse high up at the back began to wink away as I rounded the rocky point. A breakwater of massive granite blocks, two small towers flashing green and red, and then, in the gathering dusk, a harbour, large and tranquil.

Not wishing to be bothered with officials that night I moored to the northern breakwater, which was the farthest from the village, whose lights I could see. I would go over there in the morning and make an official entry into Sardinia.

While eating my frugal meal I felt the boat being hauled in, and then a heavy thud, followed by two more. Grabbing my torch I stood up in the hatchway and flashed the light towards the bow. There were three men in uniform trying to keep their balance on the slightly rocking foredeck while pointing three automatic rifles at me. It all looked so ridiculous that I just stood there and laughed. Looking a little foolish they lowered their automatic armoury and walked carefully on to the cabin-top. When I said that I was English, and only spoke a little Italian, one of them started in French, which suited me a little better. "You are on your own?" he asked. "Oh yes," I replied. "Put your firearms on the deck and come below for a cup of tea." The guns were piled with a clatter on the deck, iron-studded nails ground into the white paint, and then I had all three safely below drinking sweet tea and smoking. They were three good-looking lads of about twenty to twenty-five years. Two belonged to the police and the other, dressed in a naval rating's uniform, came from the port captain.

"We thought you were either a smuggler or transport for a few bandits when you came in without lights in the dark," said one of the French-speaking police, adding dolefully, "and then you moored such a long way from the town; we have had a long walk." After that last plaintive remark, I gave him a second cup of tea and another cigarette. I promised to call at the police station in the morning, hauled the boat close into the breakwater and helped them ashore. Before leaving they warned me that a strong easterly wind had been forecast for the morning and that where I was lying would be unsafe.

The night was still and quiet, and I felt so tired that the idea of moving anywhere else was too much. Anyway, radio weather forecasts are often wrong, so off to sleep I went.

I dreamt, some time in the early morning, that I was lazily swaying on a swing. A lovely sensation, slowly up, slowly down, on and on. When consciousness returned I was still going up and down. Heavens! The wind from the east! When I looked out I saw that the rope holding my bow to the breakwater had snapped, and I was lying to my anchor, stern on to a large swell which came through the harbour entrance. The *Nova* was quite content riding over water that looked like enormous corrugated sheeting, so I had my breakfast before moving over to the eastern breakwater.

Never before have I got into such a pickle as I did on that morning. The start was all right—I went over to the shelter of the eastern side with the outboard, and dropped the anchor just where I wanted it, but before I could make fast a line from the bow to a block of concrete, standing out from the quay, the rising wind pushed the *Nova* away from it. I got up the anchor, started the motor, and tried all over again. This time the engine stopped too soon, and I had to throw out the anchor where I was to avoid drifting on to two trading schooners. After cleaning the engine's plug I tried again, but the anchor refused to budge from the bottom. I heaved until I became dizzy—no good. Then I let the boat drift across a mooring line from one of the traders while I got my breath. When partly recovered I used the motor to go dashing to every point of the compass trying to jerk the anchor loose, but it felt as though it had got hooked on to some ancient Sardinian cannon. I let the boat drift back until the bow again came across the moorning line, and then I went below to lie down.

A boat came alongside just before midday, and in it were some men off a dredger lying in the harbour. One, a young man wearing a peaked cap, spoke perfect English—he had not even been a prisoner-of-war, though it was the first thing I asked when he spoke to me. He handed over a message to the effect that the local doctor had come to see me, as the police had told him that I had been ill. I was glad to know that my bad French had been understood by the previous night's armed visitors.

"Come and lie alongside the dredger, we will tow you over there," said the peak-capped young man. I replied, "Thank you very much, that

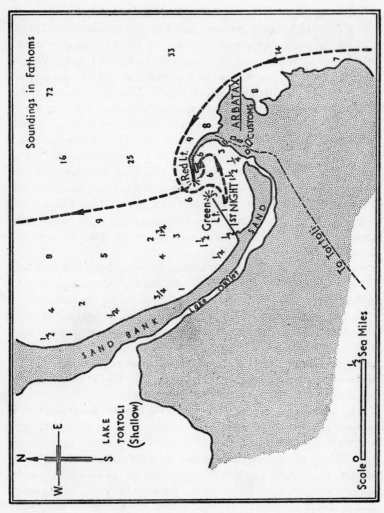

Soundings in Fathoms

72

33

14

7

16

25

8

ARBATAX

CUSTOMS

9

Red Lt.

8

6

6

3

6

9

2

1¾

3

1½

¼

1ST NIGHT 1½ ¼

Green
Lt.

5

4

½

2

¾

1

SAND

½

4

2

½

1

TO TORTOLI

SAND BANK   Late DRIFT

LAKE
TORTOLI
(Shallow)

N
W   E
S

Scale
0   ½
Sea Miles

ARBATAX

will be very nice, but perhaps I shouldn't keep the doctor waiting."
"O.K.," he said, "we'll put you ashore first, and then move you later."

A fat, paunchy doctor with a stubble of beard on his chin started asking me lots of questions which I did not understand, so I poked out my yellowish tongue at him in the hope that that was what he wanted. He shuddered and started to undress me in front of all the interested sailors leaning on their ships' bulwarks to see the fun. After examining me all over he peered at my eyes while I clutched my loosened shorts. More questions which I could not understand, so I got fed up and hailed the dredger for the English-speaking man to please come and act as interpreter. When he arrived the doctor talked rapidly to him, and then looked at me with a pleasant beam while his words were translated. I must not leave my boat. I must rest all the time. I must have white vegetables and plenty of milk. I was not going to get a "pratique" until I was better. He was going to send pills, and he was going to have some tests made from samples I had to provide.

Feeling really ill after all that I returned to the boat, and with help from the dredger moored alongside her. My anchor was recovered by willing hands, and I did as ordered and lay down on the bunk.

Some prescriptions written by the doctor were brought out to me in the afternoon. As all the dredger men had left I borrowed one of their row-boats—they had told me I could—went ashore and found a bus going to Tortoli, the nearest village. Arbatax had no chemist, only three cafés, a few houses, the police station (by far the most imposing building) and the port captain's office-cum-house.

The bus took me along a flat plain lying beneath the mountains. It was extensively cultivated with vines, maize and vegetables, with here and there a grove of cork trees. Tortoli was a compact little village, built chiefly of single-storied houses, all gaily colour-washed. It was pleasant to walk along its narrow streets and see the people. The older women all wore ankle-length black, the ones better off having white lace at wrists and neck. The girls, at least the unmarried ones, wore shorter brightly coloured skirts and low-cut round-necked blouses. They looked very pretty with their olive skins, jet-black hair, and white teeth.

The houses, I fear, must have been lousy, because stencilled on the front of each one was "D.D.T." and the date it was last sprayed.

When I found the chemist's shop I had a shock. One of the prescriptions cost the equivalent of three shillings and tenpence, the other £4. I took the cheap one and forgot the other.

When I got back to the boat, feeling dead beat, I lay down and looked at my purchase. It consisted of a row of glass phials containing an amber-coloured liquid. Looks worth the money, I thought, breaking the glass and pouring the contents down my throat.

I was sitting on a bucket when the port captain arrived. He grinned at my position, and told me that I was not to go ashore and that I was to haul up my yellow flag again. It was a nasty feeling to go up on deck and haul up the Yellow Jack—I felt like a leper must do. It was a very unhappy Violet who went to rest again.

It was blowing very hard now, and spray began to fly over the high sea-wall. Many little coasters, glistening with water, came running into the harbour for shelter. I was very glad I had not stayed at Corallo Cove, which was wide open to the east.

The cabin light was turned out early that night.

The doctor and his assistant were rowed out to me the next morning. He examined me once more, pronounced me in a very low state, and ordered me to continue to fly the yellow flag. No sooner had he gone than several of the dredger men arrived and invited me on board their boat. Nothing loth, I accepted. They took me to their messroom, and sat me down in front of a bottle of wine, saying, "Drink this, it will put new life into you." I was shown photographs of their various girl friends, wives and children. What a happy bunch they were. One, a very tall well-built fellow who came from Northern Italy, I nicknamed "Dua Metri" on the spot. This was greeted with delight, and I had to learn the names of all the others.

Because they wanted to show me where they were born I had to go back to the *Nova* and get out all the charts. The English-speaking member of the crew, Senor Piras, the second-in-command of the dredger, arrived, together with the captain, a stocky little man who gave orders as if he was taking the *Flying Cloud* round the Horn. When he heard that I was ordered to have plenty of white vegetables, he told the cook to send me over a plate of boiled potatoes every lunch-time. He also very gallantly offered to get any medicines for me, but changed his mind later when I warned him that one prescription cost 5,000 lira.

To show my appreciation I gave him a box of Senior Service cigarettes which I had hidden away for an emergency.

Senor Piras told me that the big hold-ups by the bandits had taken place near Tortoli. "Why do the police allow these bandits to remain at large?" I asked. "Because the police can't do anything about it," he explained. "The bandits are well armed, and the mountains are too full of hiding-places, and if any peasant gave information to the police he would be killed. The poor like them because many local men joined the robbers when the landowners refused to employ more than the bare minimum required to cultivate the land." It sounded like England in the feudal days.

"Occasionally," he said, "the police go up to the hills, and fire off their carbines, just to satisfy the Government in Italy."

The doctor arrived again on the morning of 11th October, and, after I had got Senor Piras to translate, I was told that he did not think I had got any infectious disease, but I must remain in port for a few days to regain my strength, and tomorrow must call at his office so that samples for bacteriological tests could be taken, for he thought I had picked up a germ in Africa.

When they had gone the port captain came and told me that I could now haul down my yellow flag. I did this with a great deal of pleasure, although I am afraid no one had taken much notice of it.

In the afternoon I decided I just could not stay any longer on the boat, and went to Tortoli. I felt so weak when I arrived that I sat for an hour or so sipping Vermouth Bianco, one of the most pleasant wines I have ever tasted. Feeling better after the wine and the rest, I wandered along a dusty road towards the mountains, past irrigated fields where bare-footed women and girls were working among the vegetables, past orange and lemon groves and solitary loquats. The fruit on some of the trees was ripe, and I felt tempted to go to a farm and ask if I might buy some, but the thought of the conversational effort involved decided me against it.

A blindfolded donkey going round an irrigation pump, the heavily laden ox-carts carrying cork and firewood to Arbatax, bare-foot boys and hungry-looking men, all brought clearly to my mind the fact that progress had not touched Sardinia very much.

Senor Piras, an obvious admirer of Mussolini, told me that when the dictator was in power a renaissance took place in the country. The peasants got more money, the dreaded malaria was almost wiped out, and there was a hopeful air about the people. Now, he said, the wealthy landowners took all they could, and let the devil look after the peasants.

Back at the port I went up to a pair of patient-looking oxen with yellowish-beige hair, and stroked their heads. I felt sorry for the poor beasts, because with the heavy oaken yoke across their necks they could not shake off the numerous flies that settled on the corners of their eyes, and could only blow away those that walked up their noses.

When I went to the doctor's house the next day my samples were taken to be sent off to the research hospital at Cagliari. Two sisters of the unmarried doctor came and talked in French to me in a shuttered little sitting-room, and before I left they presented me with a huge basket of fruit and vegetables.

While waiting for the verdict from the bacteriological people I climbed hills, drank in the local cafés, and had several meals with the dredger crew, one of whom sang opera with true Italian gusto. He was good, and I told him he ought to have lessons. The others cried me down, "No, no," they said. "We suffer enough as it is, without him practising scales while he works." Then they all imitated opera singers doing scales. I suffered again that night. Evidently raw apples and red wine were not welcome to my upset stomach.

The great day came when I was told by the port captain that I could be given "pratique." Some of the dredger men and I went to a local café for a celebration party. There I was introduced to an old skipper who was departing for Genoa with a cargo of firewood. "I'll give you a tow," he said, "until you get past the lee of the mountains." Through Piras, my interpreter, I accepted his offer, and added several "*Graciones*." Then he said, "Be ready at 3 a.m.," so I had to hurry down to the port captain's office and get that dignitary out of bed (people retire at 9 p.m. in Sardinia, except bandits and sailors) and ask him for my papers. He was most courteous, and when he handed me my signed papers he wished me God-speed and a quick recovery to the best of health. Another gesture from hospitable Sardinia.

I was ready at the time arranged by the skipper, and at 3.30 a.m. I met them outside the harbour. (Towing was not permitted because of some insurance clause, and it had to be done surreptitiously.) There was not a breath of wind outside as I fastened a heavy rope to the *Nova*'s bollard. The little green and red lights flashed a farewell to me as I was swished into the night behind the shadowy bulk of the old but powerfully engined boat ahead.

Goodbye Arbatax, goodbye Tortoli, *a riverdice.*

15

THE CROSSING OF THE FIRST LOOP

IN THE mists of early day rose the jagged peaks, always so prominent a feature of the Sardinian scene, and I could sit at ease in the cockpit enjoying their slow emerging from the cloak of night. The sea was still calm, and I waved O.K. to the old skipper standing in the stern of his ship, watching my *Nova*'s bows skim over the water in a smother of foam.

The island of Tavolara came abreast, three miles long and half a mile wide, rising to two thousand feet. One side is a cliff of pale cream coloured rock. It looked as though the island were part of an immense cheese, sliced straight down the middle.

Off Cape Ferro the wind began to blow from the south-east, and I signalled the boat to cast me off. Before doing so engines were stopped, and two sailors hauled on the tow line until we were right under their stern. Handshakes, exchange of addresses, thanks from me, and then we parted, they to Genoa, I to weave my way through the islands fringing Sardinia's northern coast.

It was my intention to go as far as Maddalena, a port on one of the islands. A fresh south-easterly was now blowing, and I had hopes of getting there before dark.

As soon as I rounded Cape Ferro and headed west I crossed the track of my outward journey, thus completing the first of the three loops that made up the voyage. Little did I know how many months would pass before I crossed the last of the loops at the Needles, Isle of Wight.

I saw coming towards me in the sunlight a sight from the olden nearly forgotten days, a square rigger with brightly varnished spars, black and white hull, and gold leaf abounding. Unfortunately she was coming up the channel against the wind, with her sails furled and relying on a diesel auxiliary. In her heyday she would have had to wait for a favourable wind.

As she came nearer, I could see many cadets and their officers on the decks. Realizing that it must be the Italian Navy training ship, I reached out my hand, unfastened the halliard of my tattered "red duster," and dipped it in salute. No sooner had I done so when whistles blew aboard, and a man raced aft to their mizen mast and returned the compliment by lowering an ensign nearly as big as the *Nova*'s mainsail. The officers and cadets lined the rails, waving and cheering. The whole business gave me a glorious feeling of elation, and sense of the camaraderie of the sea.

As she disappeared among the islands to the east, there came to my mind the picture of one of Yarmouth's notable gentlemen, a Captain Cole who, smartly dressed in navy blue with peaked cap, and with iron-grey pointed beard and searching blue eyes, is a familiar figure on Yarmouth's windy roads, walking as upright as in the days when he paced his quarterdeck in command of a windjammer roaming the oceans, when wooden ships with their towers of canvas made "iron men" and killed off the weaklings.

At 4 p.m. I was opposite Maddalena, but with the wind still in evidence, and favourable for crossing the Straits, I decided to forego a visit, and attempt a night crossing to Bonifacio in Corsica.

Of course, once in the Straits the wind, always uncertain and treacherous in these waters, dropped. It grew dark while I lay tossing on a large swell; the stars clouded over, and I knew that before long something would come, and hoped it would not blow from the north.

When the wind did come it blew hard from the north-east. I lowered the spinnaker, tied a reef in the main and, with the *Nova* hard on the wind, made a course for the light I could see on the southernmost tip of Corsica. Heavy flurries of rain began to fall. "Why," I thought, "does this have to happen to me? I am tired, and do not want to become wet as well." While I was grumbling at the weather two steamships, approaching from opposite directions, decided to try to cut us in two. I flashed my torch first at one, and then at the other, but not a bit of notice did they take. I turned and ran on a course parallel to the westward bound vessel. She was close enough to send water over the *Nova* from the bow-wave. I made a mental note to purchase navigation-lights—if some cheap second-hand ones could be found.

The absence of the low-powered light which marks the way into Bonifacio's harbour had me worried. I could see a few lights from the town high up on the cliffs, and hazarded a guess where the opening should be. Clouds and rain reduced visibility to a minimum, but when I saw a huge concave cliff looming alongside I knew where I was.

It was 1 o'clock in the morning when I made fast to the deserted quay, feeling cold, wet, and completely "tuckered in" for want of sleep, though it was very satisfying to have got so far in the past forty odd hours.

Warm golden sunshine filtered down the cabin when I woke up. I drew the blanket over my face, but soon it was too hot, and I threw it off. Two cups of tea, a piece of stale toasted Italian bread, and I was ready to face the wide-awake world. Before I could get ashore young Jacques the baker jumped on board with a thud, and was very pleased to see me again, for rumours around Bonifacio had already consigned me to a watery grave. Going ashore together we rounded up the Capitalist and the Navigator (back again on holiday) and went into their favourite poky little café for a drink. I had Mattei's Cap Corse aperitif, rich, full bodied and entirely to my liking.

Jacques admired my fawn gaberdine jacket I had bought years ago in Bermuda. I took it off there and then and offered to give it to him. "No, no," he said, rather taken aback. "Let me buy it." "How much?" I asked. "2,000 francs." "Too much, it's not worth it." "1,500 francs." "If I wasn't so broke I'd insist on giving it to you." "Well, 1,000 francs." "You can have it for 800 or forget it." He counted out 800 francs, gave them to me, and I handed him the jacket, very well pleased to have got anything at all. I later sold him some copper paint for another 600 francs, and felt really rich again. I went up to the walled town above, and bought a good supply of fruit and vegetables. The town, as before, fascinated me, and I spent several hours roaming its streets, discovering many works of art in stone or wood on the ancient houses.

Back on board I cooked myself a mammoth dish of vegetables and went to sleep, waking up in the evening to make a tour of the cafés with my friends.

Jacques' aunt and uncle owned the shop where he was baker, and he took me to meet them. The old lady, looking kind and matronly, insisted that I should eat with them, saying a solitary man did not feed properly—look how thin I was—the wind would soon blow me home again. I did not wish to take advantage of their generosity, but I was not allowed to refuse. Alas, that night, after a wonderful meal of thick soup, pork chops, vegetables and fruit, I was ill again.

Next day I explained to the kind old lady, with great deference, that I had been ill, but was careful to tell her that I had been suffering from my trouble since leaving Africa, having picked up a germ there. "Oh M. Violet, today you must come again and I will give you something to make you better, and some food that will be easy for you." Thanking her, I returned to the *Nova* to collect my petrol cans, for this was a day when it was possible to get duty-free petrol, impossible to obtain in Italian or African territories. Duty-free petrol for boats came to two shillings and a penny per gallon in Bonifacio, against six shillings for the motorist.

Gathering together all the tinned foods I had left in the *Nova*, and putting them into a sack in case the customs police came along, I took them up to Jacques' aunt. She did not want to take them, but I explained that I would feel embarrassed if all the generosity was one-sided. A herbal brew was handed over; as it was going down I realized that it was the same as the one old Dominic had once given me—very soothing to wrecked stomachs. The promised "special diet" followed—clear soup and vegetables.

The weather began to break up, strong winds and torrential rains preventing much movement about the countryside. I was introduced to a Mrs. Peyton, an Englishwoman by marriage, with French parents who lived in a flat above the customs house. She invited Jacques and me to tea, but unfortunately the tea she used had gone mouldy, so to remove the taste she gave us a glass of locally brewed "eau de vie." It might just as well have been nitric acid from the way it burned down my throat.

The next day Mrs. Peyton took me up to the town on a sightseeing tour. Going to the now practically deserted end of a rocky spur of Bonifacio where Napoleon had built enormous barracks and gun emplacements, she led me to a small building where olives were turned into oil. Apart from a motor-driven compressor nothing had been changed for hundreds of years. The olives were first ground into pulp, any oil emerging at this stage being caught in small barrels; then the pulp was put under presses and left there for several days until all the oil was squeezed out. It was then stored in huge earthenware crocks, similar to the type in which I had always imagined Ali Baba and his Forty Thieves used to hide. They held about fifty gallons each. One was cracked, and if there had been room for it in the *Nova* I would have made a bid for it.

Two very old men were there getting everything ready for dealing with the year's crop. After we had thanked them for taking so much trouble to explain the various processes to us, we walked out into the bright sunlight and headed for the room used by Napoleon when a mere lieutenant. It stood above a gateway which was rapidly decaying into rust and debris. The diminutive room had a balcony, and I tried to picture an intense young man glowering out and planning his ambitions, but nothing would emerge from the air of neglect brooding over what had once been a bustling barracks. We peered through some of the heavily barred windows, and saw signs of their use by the Italians and Germans during the war, for we could see aeroplane silhouettes painted on the walls. Next we visited a huge shaft, sunk to reach fresh water during the occupation by the *Grand Armee*. A circular stairway had been built round it and we started to go down, but it became so dark that we had to turn back. Mrs. Peyton told me that there was an opening on to the cliff-face lower down, about fifty feet above the actual level of the water, which in spite of its proximity to the sea was quite fresh. "No one would dream of using it, though," she said, "for down there go all the unwanted babies and victims of vendettas." "Ugh," I replied, "are they still as cruel and fierce as that?" "Oh yes," she answered. "Only last year a young girl tourist was found floating in the sea bound and gagged; she had been foolish enough to go out alone with a few strange Corsicans." She continued, "I have no doubt that there are many corpses lying in the harbour, weighed down with rocks in canvas bags, but no one talks or complains to the police."

This was a revelation to me, for I had thought vendettas were a thing of the past. Going into a graveyard gave me a shock, for all the coffins were either visible or cemented over, some lying in stone shelters where framed photographs of the departed were on view. Everywhere, inside and out, were violet coloured wreaths. This type of thing seems to be peculiar to the Latin countries. The wreaths stood from two to three feet high, made of fancy lattice-work of wood or metal, always the startling violet and sometimes further adorned with artificial flowers. The place looked tawdry and untidy to me.

We passed the ruins of an eleventh century monastery, and sat on a wall opposite the monks' chapel, which was still usable, a service being held there once a year. The conversation turned to local superstition, and Mrs. Peyton said, "Now I'll tell you about something that happened only the day before yesterday. A woman, who lives in one of the cottages that line the steep road-cum-steps that lead to Bonifacio, had a large running sore on her foot. The doctor gave her ointment but nothing would cure it, so she went to an old woman—the equivalent of our old-time witches—who lives on the quay near your boat. The old woman told the sufferer to come in, and sat her down at a table. Then she went out, returning in a few minutes with a cup of clear, but strong-smelling liquid. She made the woman gaze into it, and then added, drop by drop, an aromatic oil; then they both stared at it for quite a while with the old witch murmuring under her breath. When it was all over she turned to her patient and told her that a departed member of the family was very unhappy, and the soul was asking her to light a certain number of candles and say prayers for it. The woman went away and did as she was told." Mrs. Peyton added with a slight note of awe, "I saw that foot yesterday, it's now healing perfectly."

On the way back down to the quay we met the town mayor. He was distressed about the way in which the ancient town was becoming depopulated because most of the young men were going away, some to France, others to places where there was industry of some sort. "Here," he said, "we have nothing for them but fishing or a little shop work." While he was speaking I gazed back at the impressive ramparts, tufted here and there with grass, surrounding what was once the proudest town on Corsica, now useless to its inhabitants, and only a sight for summer tourists.

There was a heavy downpour that night during a violent thunderstorm. In the morning a corpse was hauled out of the harbour, shot through the head.

I too had murder in my heart that day. A man I had noticed several times before was going round selling fish from a wicker basket tied to a donkey. He had earned my intense dislike because he was always switching the puny beast. This particular morning he was cruelly personified. His moke was ill or tired out, and began to stagger, finally coming to a standstill opposite the *Nova*. I saw him raise a bottle and strike the animal between the ears, then kick it with all his might in the stomach. I shouted at him in English, forgetting all my French in my indignation, "Stop that, you bloody beast." He glared incomprehendedly and went on with the kicking. In a blind fury I picked up a hammer from the cockpit and strode over to him, collecting myself sufficiently to say in halting French, "You are a bad man, if you put your foot on the animal again I will strike you." He gently put a toe on the animal's side and I raised the hammer, then he gave me a nasty leer and walked into a cafe, amid the derisive laughter of the onlookers. I went back to the boat white and shaking.

I told Mrs. Peyton about this episode. She knew the man, and had once spoken to him about the same thing. "These people," she continued, "don't understand animals or that they are capable of feeling pain, and if they did that wouldn't stop them, for Corsicans are notorious for their cruelty." Not all, I thought, remembering the baker's family, and the love and care lavished on their dog and two cats.

Mrs. Peyton took me up to the baker's shop and bought me some "bread of the dead," saying, "This is something you must have now you're in Corsica; it's eaten at burials, and is made of sweet dough, walnuts and raisins. I learned more of Bonifacio from Mrs. Peyton, who had exiled herself there to be in the sun. The Romans made use of the natural harbour; the town remained unfortified until 1100 A.D., when the Duc de Bonifacio, a Genoese, was sent to exterminate a bunch of pirates who had taken over after the Roman departure. He built the huge outer walls, using the labour of African and Spanish slaves, and claimed the territory for the Genoese. Napoleon was born of Genoese and Italian parents. So much for nationality.

While storm-bound I went for solitary walks on the coarse land above the cliffs. The stony ground was covered with sweet-smelling herbs, among which grew the blue-flowered rosemary. Further inland there were signs of fields surrounded by crumbling walls, but nothing grew there except shrubs and brambles. No matter where I went it was the same; under the hot sun everything and every place wore an air of neglect. All the houses lacked colour-wash and looked dilapidated. Sadness and bitterness were in the air.

On 23rd October it was still blowing hard and I decided to have a really luxurious day. I climbed down some stone steps cut into the southern cliff, reached a narrow strip of beach, and spent the whole day sunbathing, eating fruit, and drinking wine. I must admit that I felt more like my old self in the evening, and looked forward to another sea-trip. The next day it rained, and once more I delayed my start, but the day after the wind eased, and before breakfast I went up to my baker friends and told them I was leaving. "Don't go," they said. "Stay here, buy a house, bring your wife and children." As I turned to go the baker's wife thrust a small parcel into my hand. After thanking them all I promised to come back one day and bring the family, even if it was only for a holiday.

16

MISTRALS

By 11.30 a.m. I was out of the harbour and under the lee of the cliffs, from which the wind came fitfully.

Round the southern tip of Corsica is a maze of reefs and rocky islands, and through them meanders a narrow channel, well marked with posts. It was an interesting piece of navigation, made easier for me by a pleasant quartering wind. At one place I had to keep two posts in line astern. This was hard to do, for every time I tried to bring the boat back in line I pushed the tiller the wrong way, only realizing my mistake when I saw the gap between the posts widening.

It was a glorious morning, cool and bracing. The ever changing spectacle of gulfs, bays, cliffs, rocks, islands and mountains held me spellbound.

As I neared the Gulf of Porto Vecchio I saw a coastal boat piled up on a rock just underneath the lighthouse. This was a boat Jacques had been telling me about. It had happened three or four nights before, during the torrential downpour. The captain and two members of the crew threw overboard a bale of cork from their deck cargo, jumped in after it, and were promptly blown far out to sea. It was two days before they were picked up, completely exhausted. The others had stuck to the ship and were there only one night. I passed within a few yards of the wreck, and was amazed to see how far it had climbed up the rock, for only the stern remained in the water. I could see what must have happened; the skipper was obviously aiming for the narrow channel between the lighthouse and the rock; then, confused by the rain, he must have turned and tried to reach the wider channel, only to find the rock in the way.

Instead of beating down the gulf to Porto Vecchio I headed for St. Cyprian's Bay at the northern head. It was large, about a mile across at the widest part, and there were plenty of nooks and crannies to make a safe anchorage for a boat of my shallow draft. After much manoeuvring and rock-dodging I found a perfect haven. No sign of life and, just ahead of me, a lovely beach behind which I could see part of a lake with its overflow running into the sea. As at my first anchorage in Sardinia there was a ruined tower; this one was perched on a hill above a grove of cedars. Not a sound disturbed the peace, save an occasional plaintive cry from a land-bird and the lapping of baby waves against the planking of the boat.

Sitting in the cabin by lamplight I suddenly spotted the parcel given to me by the baker's wife. The kind old soul had wrapped up two slabs of chocolate and a box of cheese. The simple gift brought to my mind the many occasions during my voyage when chance acquaintances had shown great generosity with no thought of anything in return.

Early next morning I watched the sun bathe the mountains in a rosy light; the lonely bewitching beauty of my surroundings held me enthralled. The sight of an open shell in the sea below, reflecting the light above from its mother-of-pearl interior, made me covetous; I plunged overboard and swam down through crystal clear water, grabbed it, and came up to the surface with lungs nearly bursting. To my chagrin the shells once removed from their watery environment looked very ordinary. I kept one half and threw the other back into the sea.

Just before dusk I cast out the spell that had hung over me all day, weighed anchor, hauled up the sails, and set off for another bay higher up the coast, called Piranello. Once outside the shelter of the bay the wind pounced on me and gave me a good shaking until I found shelter and anchored a few yards from the shore. Even there the *Nova* felt uneasy with the occasional puffs coming off the land, making her swing backwards and forwards on her anchor. I could see very faintly a group of cottages higher up the bay, but no lights were visible.

There was an altogether different feeling about this bay compared with the one where I had spent the previous evening. I slept badly and uneasily, and was very glad to see the sky colour in the east again. Before the sun was above the horizon I was on my way once more. Passing close to the cottages I could see nearby a graveyard with monstrous headstones nearly as high as the cottages, which still showed no signs of life.

Before I got out of the bay the wind dropped; there was an hour's calm, and then it blew directly from the north, down the coastline I hoped to follow. It was useless plugging into the short steep seas brought by this change of wind, and I got into another cove at the northern end of the bay.

During a cruise I have one dread, that of being caught on a lee shore in a gale. The stormy winds may blow when I'm far from land and, up to now, have not worried me unduly. From where I was to Bastia port there was not a scrap of shelter of any kind if the wind went easterly and blew a gale. I was anxious to get a favourable wind so that I could do it in one day, for it was only fifty miles to the north. During October and November the winds are tricky and fierce in that part of the Mediterranean. Nearly all the small sailing schooners lie up from mid-October.

At half-past ten the wind died again, but came to life at eleven and, praise be, blew from the south-east. Up went my faded sails and off we went along that unfriendly stretch of the coast. I had not seen a human being since leaving Bonifacio, and wondered if all the coast up to Bastia had been abandoned.

It was a wearying day trying to make the best of a tiresome wind which blew now fresh and now cats' paws. By 8 o'clock it was black night but I had made Alistro Light, thirty miles from my last anchorage.

Then the wind swung to the north and put a stop to further progress, for I was too tired to try beating against it, so turning in my tracks I made for a slight concavity in the coast just south of the lighthouse. It was so dark I could not see the shore until I was almost on it. The anchor was dropped in a hurry, and with the noise of surf all around me I had a few hours of fitful rest. Off again at six in the morning, I was only too glad to get away from such a dangerous anchorage.

Another calm descended over the sea; the sun shone warmly and I saw an ox-cart plodding along a road which ran above the shore opposite. I was able to relax and enjoyed a sun-bathe while waiting for the wind.

Far away in the distance the sea-water, reflecting the sky, changed to a deeper blue as a breeze, stealing across the surface, broke up the mirror-like surface. It forked and left me in a cleft of calm. These were just the heralds; the main body of the wind arrived soon after from the south-east. Up went all sails and the *Nova* scudded up the coast to Bastia. A glorious sail with the spinnaker pulling like a team of horses. By late afternoon I was abreast of Bastia, and after lowering the spinnaker I sailed between the two light towers of the old harbour, turned sharply to starboard and moored the *Nova* among some fishing-boats, safe and secure. Three-quarters of the way round the port were tall, narrow houses, looking like gaunt beggars gazing at a bright coin lying in a drain.

The evening sky was covered with "mares' tails," and when night came stars bleared through a heavenly haze. There was no dew. All these signs spoke of bad weather to come, and I was glad to be tied up to a heavy bronze ring embedded in a stone which must have weighed several hundredweight.

Bastia is built on a slope beneath barren looking mountains. The next morning I stalked up its narrow streets, where the shabby tenement houses leaned so close together that it would be possible for occupants of opposite rooms to watch each other eat and carry on a conversation without much raising of their voices. Between these confining walls the air was heavy with the scent of garlic and urine, and I was glad to emerge suddenly into a large square filled with stalls of fruit, vegetables and dark-looking meat. I bought some locally grown figs, oranges and vegetables very cheaply. The meat, cooked or fresh, was too dear for me.

At 4 p.m., without any warning, the wind shrieked its way down the mountains, picked up the surface waters of the harbour, turned them into swirling dervishes and carried them out to sea. I had never seen a wind blow so hard or so suddenly, except perhaps in short Gulf Stream squalls, but this wind persisted for twenty-four hours before it began to abate. I would not have given odds on the chances of *Nova*'s survival had we been out in it near a lee shore. It was the first of the winter mistrals, cold and fierce, and it kept me awake most of the night, for the anchor out at the stern kept dragging, and then the bow would bump up against the quay.

During my wanderings about Bastia I saw a man sticking up posters; he was not in the least bit particular where he put them, as often as not they were smack in the middle of a girl's face advertising perfume, or on telegraph poles. The message he was giving the world read as follows:

WORKERS!!!!!!

M. Pinay same as the Vichy Government, but instead of selling us to the Germans, is delivering France to the Americans, and consequently the French worker as cannon fodder. GO HOME AMERICANS!!!!!!

As I followed down the twisting street, plastered on either side with the work of the diligent bill-poster, I came across two policemen; they too were very busy, tearing down the warning to the workers. It seemed an awful waste of time on both sides.

I thought the previous night had been noisy, but it was comparatively peaceful when contrasted with the racket I endured the next night. First a thunderstorm hung over the town with a sound accompaniment like an ack-ack barrage, and then it began to hail. With ice pellets up to half-inch diameter bouncing on the three-eighths of an inch ply deck two feet above my sleepy head, it was like being inside a drum, with many energetic drummers trying to see who could produce the most bangs. This happened at frequent intervals throughout the night. It was cold too.

November 1st I woke late, making up for time lost during the hail-storms. The state of the past few days' weather made it very apparent to me that I ought to cut across to the South of France in the first settled interlude, but before then I had to get another chart, and the only place I could get one was off a friendly steamer in the new port. I walked past some pretty flower gardens under large, shady trees and up to some men playing bowls in a dusty road where hazards such as stones and slopes improved the game. I paused for a while to watch, for obviously this was a battle of experts. First a small metal ball was thrown seven or eight yards away; then each player of the opposing teams (any number a side) would try to place a metal ball, about the same size as a cricket ball, as near as he could to the smaller one. If an opponent's ball was in the way the next player would dispatch his own with all his might to scatter it. It looked good fun, and a game which drew devotees from both well-to-do and blue-jean clad labourers.

When I arrived at the port I spotted a new-looking Dutch steamer. Spurning the rest of the dilapidated ships lining the quay I thought

"That's the boy for me." When alongside I noticed a welder fixing a patch over a jagged hole. After climbing up the gangway I asked a tall blonde seaman for the captain—that is a word understood in any language. He led me to a door, I knocked, and a voice replied *"Entrez."* Inside was a small balding man doing accounts, who looked up, startled, and then said in English, "Good morning, sir, what can I do for you?"

That took me aback, but I was relieved to know that I could do my bargaining in my own language. "How did you know I'm English?" I asked. "That's easy," he replied. "I'm used to meeting varied nationalities; you have English written all over you." I asked him how his ship was holed; he said that he was coming into harbour in the middle of the mistral, compelled to keep at half-speed to make any progress at all. His anemometer (instrument for measuring wind force) had gone up to maximum and then stuck. The pilot lost his head in the middle of the harbour and wanted to take the boat out again; while he was dithering the ship began to drift towards the outer wall, an anchor was dropped as soon as the danger became apparent but it was too late, for though the bow was held clear the stern swung round on a partly submerged wreck which holed it. When I asked him what he thought must have been the force of the wind, judged from the anemometer reading, he hazarded a guess that it must have been seventy knots or over.

When asked if he had a chart from Rade d'Agay and San Remo he said he was not sure, but he would hand me over to the navigator. The latter searched through a large pile of charts to find the one I wanted, and when he succeeded said he had to see the captain again to find out whether it was wanted and if I could buy it; unfortunately the skipper had gone ashore in the meantime so, promising to return later, I left.

Back at the boat I decided to cook up a really special meal. First I put two handfuls of split green peas into a saucepan of boiling water; half an hour later I added some ripe figs chopped up finely; half an hour after that some fat salt bacon, also finely chopped; three-quarters of an hour later I added some left-over boiled potatoes and half a teaspoon of salt, cooked the lot another ten minutes, then scooped the now nearly solid mess on to a large plate. It was delicious, though extremely filling.

Feeling as though I needed a walk after my sumptuous repast, I first went to the end of the sea-wall guarding the old port to look at a *chasse* let into the side. Two lighted candles were guttering in the wind. They were placed under a tablet commemorating some fishermen who had lost their lives at sea. A few bunches of dead flowers lay on a floor covered with drippings from candles. It was a pathetic sight.

I started to wander up the town, but as I passed the customs house I was called inside. Wondering what was the matter I gave the two men in charge a courteous greeting, and asked why they wanted to see me. They laughed and replied that they wanted to talk, as the people round about were curious to know why I chose to sail around alone. I explained that I did it because I liked it, adding that if I had a companion we should probably only quarrel. They put forward the same old remark that I ought to have a woman to look after me, and I reflected that the Mediterranean people always think a man cannot look after himself. Aloud I replied, "A woman's place is in the home, unless she likes a seafaring life as much as I do."

They asked me where I was going to next. "Direct to Cannes," I replied. At that they became quite serious, and tried to persuade me to go first of all to the Isle of Capriaia, then Leghorn in Italy, and from there round the coast to Marseilles. I thanked them for their concern and set off once more for the Dutch ship. When I was nearly there I met the captain and the navigator coming towards me. The captain said, "You can have the chart you wanted; give the money to the quartermaster, he is looking after it for you." He paused and then added, "Take my advice and go to Leghorn first, hundreds of small craft have been lost in the Gulf of Genoa; it is a very bad piece of water in winter time." "I shall end up by becoming scared and go to Leghorn soon," I thought, then consoled myself with the thought of many gales the *Nova* had weathered in the North Atlantic.

The chart I got from the quartermaster showed in detail a hundred miles of the French south coast, with many harbours and lights. "Damn it," I said. "plenty of places to run into if bad weather comes; what is there to be scared about?"

The morning of 5th November was sunny and quiet, with hardly any wind at all. This was it—just the weather for a nice easy run of a hundred miles or so. Running back from the bakers' where I had bought

H

a couple of loaves I bumped into the harbour master. "What hurry," he said, "are you leaving today?" "Yes," I replied, "I leave at once." "Don't go direct—take my advice and go via the Isle of Capriaia, Leghorn, and follow the coast. Remember it's November." Groaning inwardly I managed to smile and say, "Good advice, I shall take it, perhaps."

Outside the harbour there was not enough wind to blow me along at the speed I wanted, so I put on the outboard to help the sails. Looking back at Bastia sprawling up the slopes beneath the hills I came to the conclusion that, although the old part of the town was an interesting study of an ancient Corsican port, I had not enjoyed myself particularly, for there I had not made any but casual friends. Besides, everything had been expensive, except perhaps the vegetables. It was a place and its people spoiled by the summer influx of visitors from the mainland.

For the rest of the morning and the afternoon the light wind prevailed. The scenery was magnificent. The wild-looking mountains jumbled down to the northern tip of Corsica, ending in steep cliffs, rocky islands, and tiny semi-circular dark-coloured beaches.

At 4 p.m. I passed the Isle of Giraglia, with its fine lighthouse. Now nothing lay between me and France, and I laid a course for Ville-franche, a port that had been described to me as one of the best on the coast. The wind by now had dropped away completely, but the outboard was purring happily and pushing me along in grand style. Two hours after nightfall the air came to life in long gentle sighs from the south-west. I set my sails to catch them and help the motor, which had then been running for twelve hours. The light from astern on Giraglia seemed to wink at me in encouragement, as though to assure to me that I would soon be across the much-maligned gulf.

By 9 p.m. the wind had settled down to a steady moderate force. The outboard was no longer needed, so I turned it off and hauled it aboard. It had served me well, and once it was secure in the cockpit I couldn't help giving it a pat of approval.

From then on the wind slowly and relentlessly increased, and by 1 a.m. I had to tie in a reef. It annoyed me by veering more to the west-ward so that I could only just hold on my course by hardening in the sheets as much as possible. The seas became large and steep, cold spray began to sweep the boat. But it was the sight above me, illuminated by a late-rising moon, that made my morale sink and droop like the barometer in the gyrating cabin. Under feathery cirrus clouds, tinged with red where the moon shone through, black wispy clouds were racing past, their edges purpled as they streaked across the face of the moon. "If it begins to blow like that down here," I thought, "I'm in for a really bad time."

On through the night we raced, overpressed by wind and wave. As the hours passed I looked more keenly ahead for the gleam of a lighthouse. At 5.30 a.m. I was thrilled to see one; clambering on to the cabin-top and holding tight to the thrumming stays I faced its direction. There it was again—two flashes that time, three the next, then one, for when in a trough I would miss some. Eventually I decided it was three flashes every twelve seconds, and went back into the cabin to find a light that followed this sequence. Back and forth I went, up and down the coast, but there was not one to be seen. This plunged my spirits to the depths, for here I was dashing towards a strange coast with no charts, in heavy seas, and a yachtsman's gale about my ears.

Realizing I should soon need all my reserves I decided the best thing to do was to have something hot to drink and eat some food. Holding the kettle on to the wildly swaying gimballed stove (the *Nova* was lurching to starboard so much that the stove went beyond its limit and kept crashing against the side), I managed to get some water hot enough for a cup of coffee. Between sips I crammed down as much bread and butter as I could manage. When I had finished I went back to the cockpit and the spray. The most glorious sight I have ever seen greeted my tired eyes. Above and beyond a dark unlit coast the sun, still below the horizon from my viewpoint, was bathing the summits of the snowy Alps in flamingo tints, shading down to the opaqueness of the night-enshrouded lowlands. I stood spellbound until the sun rose above the horizon amid a dark wrack of cloud. The coast ahead became distinct, and three clusters of white about five or six miles apart looked like towns. I could not make the one to westward with the big broken seas running, so concentrated on the middle one. Although the *Nova* was rushing through the water at a good speed the coast neared with maddening slowness. A tall slender lighthouse was the first definite object I sighted of the town I was approaching, but when still nearer my heart sank, as an unbroken line of surf could clearly be seen. With something like despair I turned eastwards, for it was hopeless to try any other direction. The wind was now astern and I fairly scudded along the rocky coast. After no sleep for thirty hours I was tired out, very cold, and extremely frightened about the future of both of us—principally the *Nova*—uninsured!

Rounding a small headland in a flurry of rain I was greeted by a sight at that moment more precious than anything else. It was the long stout arm of a mole in front of a fair-sized town. Where the channel was I did not know, but the water I went through amidst tumbling waves was shallow, for it was mixed with sand from the bottom. Then steering a sharp turn to port I found myself in calmer water in the lee of the mole. I could see the inner entrance to a port on the land, but decided to anchor where I was, and get some sleep before finding out my whereabouts and meeting customs and police.

There was to be no rest for the weary, however, for the wind blowing over the top of the mole proved too strong for my anchor, and we began to drag across a bay. I blasted everything in sight, and dropped the heavier anchor over. Then I decided I did not like the slight swell coming in, and thought it better to go into the small harbour I could see. After a back-breaking ten minutes hauling up both anchors I sailed in under jib and mizen, made a tour round inside, then picked a berth under a high quay where the wind could no longer reach me. A moment later I regretted my decision, for a shower of stones and dirt blew down on top of us. But worse things were to happen before I was allowed to close my eyes.

17

WESTWARD AGAIN

A couple of idlers came to stare at a little bedraggled sail-boat flying a torn and faded British flag and an equally torn and faded club burgee. When a man, haggard and red-eyed, asked them where he was, they got a good laugh. "Porto di Imperia; now where the hell is that?" I wondered; it was surely in Italian territory if language was any guide.

I was not left long in doubt, for a tall lean man, dressed in naval uniform, came down to the *Nova* and asked for my papers and passport. I said to him, "Please, I'm very tired; may I sleep first?" "Where have you come from?" he asked. "From Corsica," I replied. "What courage," said he, looking wonderingly at the boat. I did not tell him that before him stood someone who recently had been very frightened. I do not think he understood my request to be allowed to sleep, for he insisted on my going with him at once.

Mine was the only boat in that splendid port except for two motor-yachts laid up for the winter, and a few row-boats. Yet when I arrived at a large square building and climbed upstairs with my escort I was amazed to see that it was a hive of industry on all three floors. When seated at a table an interpreter was found, as I had failed to answer all the questions fired at me. Did they think I was a smuggler or worse? After giving such details as my place of birth, my father's name, his age (unknown to me, but I made a quick guess), I was asked for a thousand lira for charges. I slowly and carefully explained that I had no Italian money, and that in any case I had been in many ports in the Mediterranean, including several Italian ones, and had never yet had to pay any charges. Furthermore I had only come to their port under duress from the weather. It was no use, they wanted a thousand lira, it was necessary for me to pay the charge. By now I felt in an evil mood, and leaving all my other papers on the table I grabbed my passport and walked out in a temper, leaving them looking rather astonished. To my relief no attempt was made to detain me by force. I marched down the street, across the quay, hauled in the *Nova*, scrambled aboard, and went to sleep.

In the evening I walked along a road bordering the sea until I came to another town and port. It was an older place than Imperia; its shops, well-filled, were recessed under colonnaded pavements, so that would-be purchasers could loiter and gaze at their merchandise in the shade. Even though it was 8 p.m. most of the shops were still open. I went into a food shop which was packed tight with all kinds of delicacies like smoked ham, liver pâté, black and green olives, and many different types of cheese. Waving a five hundred franc note under the nose of a bald-headed rotund little man behind the counter, I pointed to a cheese which caught my fancy and said, "O.K.? *Dua centa gramme*." He took the note, held it up suspiciously to the light, crinkled it with his fingers and then, satisfied, he smiled, nodded his head, and weighed me up two hundred grammes of cheese. I got back some Italian coins in change, so with them I went to another shop and bought two loaves of bread.

Now that I had solved the food problem I walked back to Imperia, had a snack on board, and went to sleep again.

When I awoke next morning I found two policemen standing on the quay above the boat. As soon as they spotted me I was beckoned ashore. My passport had to be stamped, and with a policeman each side of me I went to their headquarters. No trouble here; a few questions, a rubber stamp, nothing to pay, and I was allowed to go.

For the rest of the day I wandered round Imperia, explored a lovely old church, and watched a most curious game being played by some of the young bloods of the town. On a rectangle of rough ground, about the size of a tennis court, were four men, two on each side. A heavy rubber ball was served by being hit, with a bandaged fist, to the side of a house alongside, allowed to bounce once before being hit back again via the wall to the other side. The force with which they sped the ball from one side to the other was tremendous, and called for much vitality and skill.

Standing among the watching crowd, a man next to me gave a running commentary. I could not understand him at all, but kept nodding my head as a form of encouragement to keep it up. When the game was over I said "Good-day" in my best Italian and walked off, feeling like one of the populace.

On 8th November the wind had abandoned its westerly violence and was blowing gently from the east. A good day to go westward. With some trepidation I decided to tackle the port authorities.

Passing the armed sailor on guard at the entrance to the port building, I climbed up the stairs and politely asked for the interpreter. When he arrived I told the rather sour-looking officer that I wished to leave. To my consternation I was now asked for five thousand lira. In vain did I protest and demand a reason for the increase, so I dug in my toes and said flatly, "I won't pay; I've no money, and even if I had I don't see why I should pay." More and more men gathered round the table, some in sailors' uniform and some in civilian clothes. I was asked to wait while my case was discussed with higher authority. The minute-hand of a clock high up on the wall slowly ticked off the minutes. When twenty had passed I got up and left, calling at the police office to get an exit stamp on my passport. Again this proved quick, and the man responsible for the stamping was interested in my wanderings.

For the third time I went back to the port captain's building with the intention of having a battle-royal. When I reached the room upstairs I saw my papers lying on the table. In the corner was a rating pounding a typewriter. I picked up the papers and said, "Do I have to pay?" He smiled and replied, "No, no money." Feeling very relieved I dashed down the stairs and along to the boat, which I immediately got ready for sea. In less than ten minutes I was sailing out of the harbour, which though a delightful haven had been spoilt for me by my first and only dispute with officialdom.

While at the police station earlier in the morning I had been told that Mentone, the first French port, was only forty miles to the west and San Remo in between. I was hoping to reach Mentone before the end of the day. The light easterly wind was ideal for the spinnaker, and we made good speed in spite of the swell still rolling up against us.

In the bright sunshine it was delightful sailing, in sight of a shore that looked rugged and interesting, with terraced hills, dotted with gaily coloured villas, dominating the skyline. The Alps I had seen on the wild ride from Corsica were hidden from view, much to my disappointment.

The pleasant wind was too gentle to last, and faded away two or three hours after leaving Imperia, but the lumpy sea persisted. I had no intention of waiting off the rocky coast for the wind to return, so as I had enough petrol on board to get me to San Remo, now only ten miles away, I put the outboard on the stern and started motoring. It was slow going with that sea running, but its steady push got me in sight of San Remo within a couple of hours. Then, fortunately, a breeze sprang up from the south-west, which saved me from running out of petrol in the harbour mouth, and ignominiously sculling in.

Along the sea-wall were several smart looking yachts, motor-cruisers and, nearer the land, some fishing craft. After a couple of tours round, looking for the most comfortable berth, I decided to join the fishing-boats and save some of the walk to the town. For once I did the mooring-up without mishap, getting the sails down in time, the anchor flung out astern the right distance from the quay, and enough momentum to bring the bow within a foot of a ring-bolt. Feeling very pleased with myself, and wishing I always managed so well, I went below for a belated cup of tea.

The authorities were much easier here. When I came up on deck there was a policeman on the quay waiting for me to put in an appearance. Passport and papers were taken away and brought back within ten minutes—nothing to pay.

Walking through the town a little later on I was impressed by its cleanliness and air of prosperity. Sheltered from the north by a curtain of hills it was degrees warmer than Imperia. No wonder it is popular amongst those of our more prosperous citizens who seek the sun in winter.

On my way back to the boat I saw two men approaching; one broke away when I was spotted and, coming across to me, said in English, "Are you off the *Nova Espero*?" "Yes," I replied.

With his voice full of jubilation he said, "My dear chap, I'm delighted to see you; I know all about your ship." My new-found acquaintance turned out to be a keen cruising enthusiast. Leaving his friend he took me to see his own boat in which he hoped to do an Atlantic crossing. It was a fine ship about thirty feet long; double-ended (pointed bow and stern) and double-planked. We had a long and interesting conversation all about boats and long sea-passages.

He also told me a good deal about himself. Polish by birth, he had escaped from his country when the Germans had smashed their small armed forces. After wandering through many countries he eventually reached England, joined the R.A.F. and became Pilot Officer Christopher Grabowski, with a burning hatred of all things Germanic. Christopher (we were soon on Christian name terms) told me he was staying with friends in the town who had offered him very generous hospitality while his boat was being fitted out. I was surprised to learn that he was married, his wife and child living with his mother and father in North Africa. When I was back in England I had a long despairing letter from him; he had had to sell his boat through lack of funds, returned to his wife, and was working somewhere near Tunis. Only a fortunate few achieve their dreams.

Chris departed for dinner and I went back to the *Nova*.

I had just finished a meal of bread, cheese and bananas when Chris hailed me from the quay with a request for permission to come aboard with a friend. I welcomed them warmly with a promise of coffee in a few minutes, and forthwith Chris and his friend squeezed through the narrow hatchway, bumped their heads on the deck beams, and sat down on the bunks. Christopher's friend turned out to be a very charming lady, the Marchesa Borea d'Olmo. They had come to take me to a party at the house of a man who acted as agent for the British firm Permuttit. The last word struck a chord in my memory, for it was that firm who supplied us with de-salting kits on our Atlantic crossing, and thus enabled us to carry more food.

Christopher had to leave us for a few minutes to get something off his boat. The Marchesa turned to me and said, "When Chris came home this evening he flung open the door and said, 'Guess who's here! Charles Violet off the *Nova Espero*.'—I confess I was completely unmoved, but now I've seen your boat and heard about her previous voyages I'm really quite glad to meet you, and I hope you will join us for dinner tomorrow evening."

The three of us left the *Nova* and walked up a broad avenue lined with palms and gardens, so brilliantly lighted that the moonlight over the sea and the shore below us seemed wan and unreal. We came to a block of modern flats gleaming with glass, black and white tiles, and chromium-plate, squeezed into an automatic lift, shot up several storeys, and entered a very pleasant apartment with subdued lighting and books everywhere. Our host and hostess, Tito Serralungo and his wife, an English girl from the Argentine, made us very welcome, although the Tito kept changing from English to voluble Italian which was far beyond the resources of my meagre vocabulary. We left in the early hours of the morning with an invitation to dinner a couple of days later. Protests from me that I must be on my way were overborne by persuasion from the entire company. The Marchesa clinched the matter by saying that her husband would never forgive her if I was allowed to leave before he returned from Rome. I was quite unable to listen to such insistent pleading without giving way, and ended up by staying a week.

Christopher and I developed a mutual exchange system. He planned to sail to Tunis before attempting the Atlantic, and I gave him many charts of the Mediterranean, and books and paint, in return for which I received tinned foodstuffs.

One day the Marchesa brought her little son and his Nanny to have tea on the *Nova*. Although only three years old he gave me a display of old-fashioned courtesy seldom seen in our modernized western world. He gave a deep bow upon introduction, and proved tractable down in the cabin, although, like any normal trumpet-blowing child, he did seem fascinated by the foghorn, but stopped when we had had enough. Another deep bow and gravely-spoken thanks were accorded me on departure.

The dinner I had at Palazzo Borea was great fun. The great gloomy old house, filled with priceless antiques, came to life that night. After dinner, during which conversation ranged from boats to God, Christopher, the Marchesa and I went to see an Italian film called "Il Capotto" (The Coat). The lead was played by an actor named Rascel, who reminded me of Charlie Chaplin—amusing, whimsically sad, and able to convey to the audience all shades of emotion with very few words. Even with my scanty Italian I could follow the whole story from the start to the sad conclusion. On the way back the Marchesa, nicknamed Bruscola (melon-seeds) wore my cream-coloured duffle coat with its three broad bands of green, red and black, much to the amusement of the passers-by we encountered on our way back to the Palazzo.

On the 14th of November I was taken ill again, but the following day I recovered sufficiently to greet the Marchese Gian Marco Borea d'Olmo, who had just returned from Rome. A tall handsome man, who had lost an arm when flying with the Italian Air Force during the war, he was a very keen yachtsman, and when I offered to take him with me on the next leg of the journey he accepted at once.

There was a party of eight for tea that day, all squashed tightly in *Nova*'s tiny cabin, which is nine feet long, six feet wide, and has only three and a quarter feet between the floors and the cabin top. There were Tito and his wife, Bruscella and Gian Marco, plus their small son with his Nanny, Christopher, and myself. A bit of swell was coming into the harbour and the very fancy cakes I had bought for the occasion were hardly touched, but after my guests had departed, some looking rather green, I rather greedily devoured the lot.

That same night I had a very unpleasant experience. On my way back to the boat after spending the evening at Palazzo Borea, where I had met Gian Marco's father, the Duke, I took a short cut along an alley linking two main streets. Half way through a man emerged from a doorway and said something to me; I did not understand him and replied, "No, no." Before I could continue on my way he socked me with all his might on the jaw. Taken by surprise, and off balance, I fell flat on my back. Although dazed I was not completely knocked out, and felt him going through my pockets. Then equally suddenly he stopped, stood up, seemingly to listen. Something had disturbed him. Lingering just long enough to give me a parting kick in the ribs, he took to his heels and disappeared down the alley. Fortunately for me he must have been wearing rubber- or rope-soled shoes, for this last attention did not hurt very much. Nobody came, and after a few minutes I stood up and was promptly sick. Returning slowly back to the boat I deliberated on whether I should go to the police or not, but when I remembered Imperia I finally decided not. Apart from a bruise on the jaw I was unharmed, and anyway the joke was on my assailant, for that night I did not have a single lira on my person; what little I possessed was in the boat.

An east wind was blowing on the 16th, and I hurriedly got in touch with Gian Marco to let him know that this was a day for departure. Having many things to do it was not until midday that he arrived, complete with rugs, fruit and wine. Christopher, who was looking a little forlorn and envious at the thought of our sailing away, said, "Some people have all the luck; I wonder if I shall really sail my boat away from here. Anyway, a pleasant trip to you both. Charles, it's been wonderful meeting you, don't forget to write to me when you reach England." Bruscola and her son were also there to see us off, and we even had a few words with a very worried Tito, whose boat had been stolen the previous evening. No one noticed the bruise on my jaw, and I did not say anything to spoil the mood of my most hospitable friends. Finally all the goodbyes were said, the sails hoisted, and we were on our way. *Nova*, for the first time since leaving England, had two men to carry for a part of the journey.

On the sea-wall, silhouetted against the background of beautiful San Remo, stood Bruscola and her little son waving their arms in farewell.

18

COASTING THE RIVIERA

THE MARCHESE, in spite of having only one arm, proved to be a very handy man in a boat, and enjoyed himself at the helm while I kept serving hot coffee, tea or chocolate, for the weather was very cold. The wind freshened during the afternoon and we bowled along in fine style, with small white horses for ever chasing us astern.

Mentone soon came abeam, gleaming whitely in the sun. Now we were in French territorial waters, and hoped on the following day to reach Cannes, which I had intended to be first port of call after leaving Corsica. After passing Cape Martin the warmth of the sun began to wane and I, hating the cold, especially on the water, voted we should stop for the night at Monaco, the port for Monte Carlo. Gian Marco agreed, but what a disappointment the harbour proved to be. The entrance was very imposing, high sea-walls ending in two graceful towers, but we were told to tie up on the western side of the port. Great mounds of coal were lying on the quay, waiting to be fed into the furnaces of an electric power-station. There was too much "slop" coming in through the harbour entrance to lie against the sea-wall, and we tied up to a dirty old oil-barge.

Gian Marco, master of several languages, soon handled the customs, police and harbour master, telling the latter what he thought of him for placing us in such an unpleasant berth, but was told that the other side was entirely taken up by yachts which spent the whole winter in the harbour.

We tidied up ourselves and the boat, and set off to see this fabulous town, where my wealthy countrymen had been pouring money into the pockets of the Casino shareholders for many years.

Gian Marco had been there many times before, and led me to a tiny bar used by yachtsmen. Unfortunately it was nearly empty, and none of his cronies was there. After a couple of aperitifs we went on to a small restaurant in the old part of the town, where we had an extremely good meal for very little money.

During a walk we took after dinner the only sight which struck me as beautiful was the long strip of ornamental garden in front of the floodlit Casino. My companion asked me if I would like to have a little flutter, but at that time I could not afford to waste a single shilling, and suggested that we had an early night instead, although inwardly I regretted my poverty, for I would have liked to have had just one gamble on the famous tables.

We got under way at 11 o'clock the next morning, but still failed to reach Cannes, for in the afternoon the wind blew strongly, and not feeling very well I decided to put in at Antibes.

We had a bit of trouble when we entered that ancient, once fortified old port. The wind blew directly against us, and I was not used to having someone to help me tack the boat. We narrowly missed a broken-down jetty, shaved a large coaster, and finally had the sails down too soon and the anchor fouled on a fishing-boat's moorings. With help from the shore we berthed at last, and I have no doubt that Gian Marco's estimate of my seamanship suffered a serious setback.

Gian Marco, who was returning to San Remo, volunteered to fetch the drinking water for me the next morning. Taking my wicker covered ten-litre bottle he walked away, after receiving instructions from me not to fill it from the nearby fountain, but at a street hydrant. When he came back I made the tea and took a sip—it was foul. I spat it out, grimaced at Gian Marco, and said, "Confess; this is fountain water, isn't it?" He laughed and admitted it was. He had found that he could not manage the hydrant and hold the bottle at the same time, so had gone across to a café and asked the woman behind the bar if she would fill it for him. No, sir, she would not. "Use the hydrant across the street," she said. So, in desperation, he had filled up with the polluted water, hoping I would not notice.

I was sorry to see my friend depart, for he had been a most pleasant companion. After he had left I wandered up to the market-place and consoled myself by gazing at all the rich display of fruit and vegetables. Not feeling like continuing on my way, and only having myself to please, I walked round the quay where many fine big yachts were tied up and continued along the sea-front where a beautifully curved beach followed the line of a rock-strewn bay. On the furthest point dark green pine trees contrasted with the rich turquoise blue of the sea. This is an ancient town set in lovely surroundings and, to my taste, far superior to the stucco and artificiality of Monte Carlo.

That night it rained and rained, thrumming on the cabin roof, stopped for an hour or so in the morning, then resumed its fall until 4.30 in the afternoon. I collected enough water in the cockpit to keep me supplied for a month had it been necessary. I baled it out and decided to go as far as Cannes; but first I had to get my passport stamped. This proved to be a very long-winded business. The first office I went to sent me to another, about a mile away, and they in turn sent me back to the first one, which dispatched me again to the second, but this time I found no one there. I walked down to the quay, picked up a customs man, and told him what was happening to me and that I was in a hurry to leave. Taking compassion on me he led me back to the original office, where a wordy battle ensued which ended in my getting my passport stamped and then being told that there would be a sanitary tax to pay. "Oh lord," I thought, jingling a few francs in my pocket. "What now?" The length, breadth and tonnage was asked for. A long calculation on a piece of paper, and then a demand was made for what I thought, at first, was eight hundred francs, but upon querying the figures several times I found to my surprise and relief that he was saying eight francs—about twopence. I paid with a smile, handed out cigarettes, shook hands with gusto all round, and left. It was dark outside, so my departure was once again postponed.

Wind and rain kept me in harbour the following day, but on 20th November the sun came out again, and I set off to Cannes. There was no wind at all outside the harbour, only a well-rounded swell that made the *Nova* curtsy to the deep blue sea. My outboard purred away merrily and I felt on top of the world—beauty, beauty everywhere and all for me to see! The crowning glory came when I reached the end of the two-mile long peninsula which juts into the sea south-east of Antibes. Looking astern I saw once again the snow-capped Alps, standing stark against the pale blue sky of a winter's day. A breathtaking sight, but the neglected *Nova* brought my attention back, by starting to turn a circle.

From Cap d'Antibes I laid a course between the island of St. Marguerite and the mainland. St. Marguerite, the inner of two islands collectively named Isle de Lerins, had a large forbidding citadel on its northern shore and a small quay to land the tourists from Cannes who swim there in summer time, for the water is very shallow right across to the mainland at Point Croisette. Going over this shallow part very slowly I could see the bottom quite plainly, through water of a greenish hue. Gian Marco had drawn for me a map of Cannes harbour, and had marked off a section which would be a very bad berth for the *Nova* if the wind blew from the east. It is known locally as the Cemetery, and lies at the end of the western jetty. Sailors beware!

Cannes harbour was packed tight with yachts of every size and description, many flying the Red Ensign. Twice I circled round looking for a niche large enough for the *Nova*, but it was useless and I had to moor at the inner end of the Cemetery, next to a 112-foot Fairmile flying the British flag. On her stern was painted in large letters *Ginasal*.

I went ashore and had my passport stamped, then walked a little while in France's "Brighton." It is a very jolly place to spend a holiday, provided one has plenty of money. Pleasant ornamental gardens, palm trees, large white buildings and an air of cheerful prosperity made it an invigorating town, with a feeling that a good time was just around the corner. I walked back along the broad quay to the *Nova*, climbed aboard, and was just about to disappear below when a voice from *Ginasal* hailed me asking, "Is that the little boat that crossed the Atlantic?"

"Yes, it is," I replied, feeling as always a little awkward when asked that question. "May I come aboard?" came the next request. "Of course," I replied, and a young man jumped aboard and introduced himself as Tim Whelpton from Norfolk, a small boat sailing-man. He had come south on the *Ginasal* as a paid hand to see the Mediterranean. After asking many technical questions about the *Nova*'s construction and sailing qualities, he told me that the skipper and his wife, a Mr. and Mrs. Davies, would like me to come aboard the *Ginasal* for a meal. Going aboard I was introduced to Mr. and Mrs. Davies; the latter looked at me and said, "Mr. Violet, you look as though you've been starving yourself for months." She turned to her husband and continued,

A beautiful statue at Marseilles

The little Dutch botter at Toulon

141

Roman theatre at Arles sur Rhone

Roman arena at Arles, now the scene of bull-fighting

142

"I think the *Ginasal* had better adopt the *Nova Espero* while she stays in Cannes, don't you?" "Why, of course," he replied. "All meals aboard here."

That night, after a meal the like of which had not come my way for a very long time, I beamed at Mrs. Davies' matronly form as she carried in the coffee, and assured her with deep feeling that her husband was a lucky man; it was a long time since I had had such a delicious supper.

The owner of *Ginasal* was away in England, but the crew, consisting of the skipper and Mrs. Davies, with their fourteen-year-old son, the engineer and his wife, and Tim, were all kept hard at work keeping such a large yacht up to scratch. The owner was fortunate to have such a conscientious man as the skipper. Below *Ginasal* was a lovely boat with beautifully decorated staterooms, a large lounge, and a cosy dining-room next to an all-electric galley.

It was a very cold night, and I began to think that winter in the south of France was not quite as described by the tourist bureaux. At 7 o'clock in the morning I brought my nose above the blankets, opened one eye, and looked at the thermometer—it was 37 degrees F., only five degrees above freezing.

During the rest of the day I was assured by many people, both English and French, that it was not usually as cold as this.

I spent a couple of entertaining hours walking round the rows of yachts. Errol Flynn's tall-masted schooner was there, next to a large ketch with upperwork of polished teak. I learned that most of the sumptuous yachts were owned by Greeks, and that they paid the highest wages to their crews. I had always thought of Greece as a poor country.

On board the *Ginasal* in the evening I met a most interesting woman. She was a Mrs. H. who lived alone in a small motor-cruiser. The passing years had left untouched her clear-cut features, and above the sharp contrast of dark eyebrows and brown eyes her snow-white hair only enhanced her beauty. She had sailed for many years, usually alone except for a dog, which had become so sea-minded that if she allowed the boat to become too close to the wind it would put its shoulder to the tiller and push until the boat once more came back "on the wind." Looking at the doubt in my face when she had told me this story she

I

said, "I was not telling a shaggy dog story; it is really true."
I believed her.

The skipper too recounted a yarn, the truth of which was vouched
for by his wife. He did not really want to tell the story as it was against
himself, but the rest of us goaded him into doing so. He and his wife
and baby had been to stay with some friends at Colwyn Bay. Soon after
their arrival, while the two of them were looking round the garden,
his friend's wife came down the path carrying a baby. He admired it,
and said that it was very much like his friend, although it had its
mother's eyes. "You great fool," cried his wife, kicking him on the
shins, "it's your own!"

Before I left Cannes Mrs. Davies presented me with an article that
proved to be my greatest comfort in the cold that I had to endure
during the next few months. It was a hot-water bottle.

On 24th and 25th November it blew a hard mistral, but on the 26th
the wind came moderately from the south-east, favourable for me.
I told Tim Whelpton that this was the day, for he had expressed a keen
desire to have a sail on the *Nova*, and I had agreed to take him. The
skipper had allowed him a couple of days off, provided that he made up
the time later. By 10.15 a.m. we were ready. I had bade farewell to all
the friends I had made, and whose hospitality I had enjoyed. Hoisting
all sail to the wind, which seemed to be dying, we crept past the
Cemetery and out into the Golfe de la Napoule, where the land sweeps
in a large curve to the south-west in a vista of tree-clad hills, golden
beaches and white villas.

We had a pleasant surprise when we were about two miles out of
Cannes, for looking astern we saw *Ginasal* come sweeping out of the
harbour and heading towards us. It did not take them long to overtake
us and soon her sharp bow, cutting water away in curving wedges, was
abreast of us. The skipper waved from the bridge, and the rest of the
crew shouted as they passed, but we could not understand what they
said. *Ginasal* slowed down after passing us, and then stopped. When we
caught up with them the skipper told us that he had decided to pump
out the bilges, a job which must not be done in Cannes harbour.
Telling us he was still too near the land, he volunteered to give us a
thrill by being towed at eleven knots. Knowing that the *Nova* tows like
a surf-boat and really planes on top of the water, I agreed. The long

tow-rope tightened, and the *Nova* lifted up her bows, sat on her stern, and whistled over the water at a thrilling speed. After a few minutes *Ginasal* slowed down, the engineer hauled on the tow-line, and when we were close up Mrs. Davies emerged from the galley and handed us two large plates piled high with food.

We sat on the *Nova*, eating and looking at the distant landscape, while the skipper cleaned out his bilges. A most enjoyable half-hour. *Ginasal* returned to Cannes while we, in a wind recovering from its midday sleep, headed westward.

We sailed past many famous places that afternoon—Rade d'Agay, St. Raphael, the Gulf of St. Tropez, and others. Off Cape Taillat we were bombed and strafed by the French Air Force. A hundred yards off the cape lies a whale-shaped rock; as we approached we saw several planes dive at it, release a bomb, and then dive away. Tim wanted me to head out to sea, but I thought of the distance wasted if we did not cut this corner, and decided that maybe they would stop when they saw us. There was a lull in the activity as we passed by the actual rock, but no sooner were we a few yards past than the planes began to swoop down again, this time firing rockets, some of which hit the rock, scattering splinters in all directions, while those which missed went ricochetting out to sea. Very exciting while we were near the rock. It was not until we were three or four hundred yards past that I noticed a large red flag flying from the cape. Then a plane broke away from those circling above the rock, and flew down towards us, passing a few feet above the *Nova*'s mast. The pilot shook his fist at us as he roared past. Tim had been right—we should have avoided that particular spot.

We headed for Lavandou, and now, well clear of the cape, we hoisted the spinnaker, a quicker job with two, and for the next few hours we had some glorious sailing along a beautiful coastline.

Darkness came before we reached harbour, and we had a tricky half-hour trying to make out which lights showed the entrance to the port. Tim had been to Lavandou once before, but he confessed that he did not recognize it as the same place at night. After one false lead we finally gained the proper entrance, and within a matter of minutes we were moored alongside the quay in five feet of water.

This port is a new one, and was still incomplete when we were there, but it will make a very safe port for shallow-draft boats, with room for those drawing up to ten feet lying along the outer wall.

Tim and I walked around the small but well-lighted town. If Cannes may be called France's Brighton, this was the equivalent of Bognor Regis. A beach of fine sand curved round the front of the town, where palms and other trees offered plenty of shade in the summer.

We set off next morning with a light west wind blowing, hoping to reach Toulon before nightfall. At first we had to head due south down the Bormes Road to Cape Benat, and consequently it was smooth going in the lee of the land. Away in the distance we could see the easterly group of the Hyeres Islands, one of which is owned by the famous French nudist colony. As we had no binoculars on board we saw nothing of interest.

Once past the cape we had to start tacking into an increasing wind against steep, wicked little seas which threw spray at us and almost stopped progress. First of all we decided to try to get to Porquerolles Island, the westerly one of the Hyeres group, but as the wind increased I got tired with the lack of progress made, and decided to sheer off to north-west towards the mainland. We had to find somewhere to land so that Tim could be put ashore, for he had strict instructions to return that night. It was obvious that we should never reach Toulon in time for him to catch a train back, so I picked out on the chart a place where I hoped he would find some means of transport back to Cannes. At least there was a light shown near a place marked in very small print— Salins Anchorage—and to this we headed, bouncing over the waves and getting wetter every minute. Slowly we worked in towards the shelter of the land, and after a series of mishaps in shallow water we eventually made fast to one of the piles of a pole pier. We climbed up and walked along some rotting planks on top, and at the landward end we came to a padlocked door surrounded by barbed wire. By going round the outside and squeezing carefully through some of the wire strands, we finally came to a dirt road with cottages in the distance. A man dressed in the usual uniform of a French worker, blue denim jacket and trousers, came slouching towards us, hands in trousers pockets. We asked him whether it was possible to get back to Cannes, but he spat in the dust and said he did not know, and then continued on his way. We then enquired of a pleasant looking woman, and she had

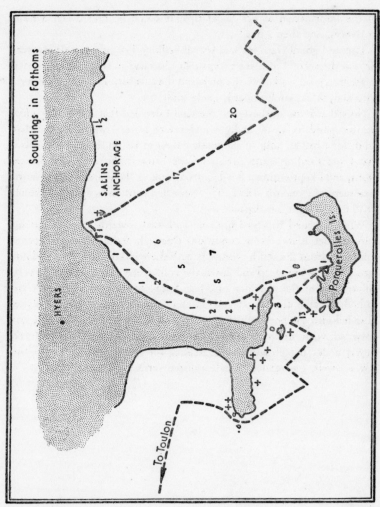

Soundings in Fathoms

HYÈRS

SALINS
ANCHORAGE

1½

2

1

1

1

1

2

2

2

6

5

5

7

17

20

7

0

3

13

Porquerolles Is.

To Toulon

SALINS AND
PORQUEROLLES
ISLES

all the information at her finger-tips. It could be done; first a walk to Hyeres, and then a bus.

Tim said goodbye to me and set off walking briskly towards Hyeres. He was the second pleasant companion I had had so far, and I was sorry to see him go. I walked to the pier, did the acrobatics round the barbed wire and, when safely aboard, made some tea.

Now that I was in the lee of the land I decided that the strong wind was too good to waste, and got under way again. I was very glad that I did, for I had an hour of the finest sailing so far on the journey. Now that I was heading south towards Cape Esterel, the wind was on my beam, and I kept within a few hundred yards of the low and sandy shore (see map), in smooth water. The *Nova* fled south at a speed of which I had not thought her capable.

When I passed Esterel I headed south-east towards the harbour on Porquerolles Island. Now conditions changed, and a huge swell came rolling up from the south-west, but with the wind free the *Nova* did not care a bit. Swishing up and down the rollers she gave me a thrill very different from the previous care-free hour. In the gathering dusk we rushed towards the island and quieter water. Guided by the lights I headed into the port, which as far as I could see in the poor light was crowded with fishing-boats. I got down the mainsail and entered slowly under the jib and mizen. Making for a clear spot alongside the low sea-wall, I grounded heavily a dozen yards from the quay.

19

SECOND LOOP COMPLETED

A FISHERMAN came to my rescue as soon as he saw that my own efforts were futile. He tossed me a line from the stern of a nearby boat and dragged me into deeper water.

I wandered aimlessly up to the village where, so I was told later, many people come to escape the summer heat of the towns on the mainland. It is a pretty place nestling among the trees which crowd the island.

I went into a café near the harbour and had a Dubonnet. A few fishermen, having, I suppose, been told of my sticky entrance to their port, engaged me in conversation, and drew maps from puddles of wine on the table, using their fingers, to show the shallow parts of the harbour, and explained what I should have done. My mood was for company and I kept raising fresh topics of conversation. The Germans? Very well behaved provided you did what they wished—if not, brutal. Fishing? Very poor just now, though prices were good. Tourists? Ah! plenty of money to be taken off them provided you could give them what they want.

Going aboard that night I made a clumsy step and went overboard. Getting out of the water was difficult for one foot remained on board caught up in a rope, but after drinking a considerable amount of the Mediterranean I made it, giving my back a nasty wrench and losing some skin from my leg. The accident puzzled me for I am usually so careful. To satisfy myself I went back to the quay and walked along a line on the concrete. Too much wine!

It was not until the middle of the morning that I hoisted the sails, and, keeping in the lee of the island as long as I could, headed for Toulon. After passing Bon Renaud Point I once more encountered the same conditions as on the day before, large rollers and a west wind. On the extreme western part of Porquerolles is a tangle of rocks, and on one of these is a lighthouse. They were a magnificent sight that sunny morning with creaming green waves breaking over them, and the low roar coming from the welter of foam reminded me of part of Debussy's "La Mer." Tacking over those humps of sea against a light wind was slow. I had never imagined the Mediterranean could produce such a swell; it was more like the Atlantic.

Past Rebaud Island I kept nearer the mainland which here juts out into the sea like an inverted "T," with the Hyeres Roads on one side and Giens Gulf on the other. As I rounded the western arm of the "T," threading my way through a maze of reefs and islands, the wind freshened and backed a little to the south-west. First, for no apparent reason, I headed due north into the centre of the gulf, then, laying a compass course, for the sun had disappeared and a mist had risen, I made due west for Toulon.

A fishing boat came into view, the first craft I had sighted that day. Now I had a real idea of the size of the swell, for, although only a couple of hundred yards away from me, her crew disappeared completely when in the trough of the seas. They gave me a friendly wave as they passed. I met the skipper later in Toulon, and he was most emphatic about the size of the waves, and pleased me with some complimentary remarks about the *Nova*.

Once well in the Grand Rade of Toulon Bay I was in calm water, but I viewed with distaste the scum and garbage, which increased as I went further in. Lord Nelson is reputed to have once said, "There are only three safe harbours in the Mediterranean—June, July and Toulon." Land-locked except to the south-east, it can easily hold a large fleet, and in the Petite Rade it is even protected from that direction by a long breakwater.

After passing the breakwater I had an unexpected thrill. A French destroyer overtook me at this point, and without moving from my seat in the cockpit I lowered the ensign from the mizen-top. A whistle blew aboard the destroyer, a sailor raced aft, and I was honoured in turn. Officers and men lined the rail grinning and waving. That made the second time a foreign naval vessel had saluted my weatherworn little boat, and it certainly gave me a pleasant feeling. I worked my way into an inner harbour for small boats, which lay right in front of the city. A familiar sight greeted my eyes for there, tied up at the best berth by some steps, was the little Dutch Boyer I had seen in Marseilles, the skipper of which had said he was going to sail to South America. He had certainly sailed a few miles, but in the wrong direction. I wondered whether he was still selling photographs advertising his proposed trip.

I was ordered out of the first berth I had chosen because it was reserved for fishing-craft. I had to move to a spot where there was about half an inch of diesel oil on top of the water and my lines and hands were soon covered with it.

The first person to greet me when I got ashore was the Dutchman himself. He was carrying a bulging sack of foodstuffs he had been given by an American ship. That man would certainly not go short of anything for want of asking. He was most hospitable and asked me to come aboard his boat for a cup of coffee, where we were joined by a charming blonde Dutch girl.

After being initiated into multifarious ways in which a world voyager can pay his way, and may get things for nothing, I returned to the *Nova*. Standing looking at her was a slightly-built military looking man whose appearance seemed vaguely familiar to me. He introduced himself as Major Kitchener. "Good heavens," I said, "now I know you, we met several times in Bermuda." Then he remembered too. He and his wife, Winnie, had sold their Bermudian island, gone to England, and bought a fine ketch, *Sentinel II*. The yacht had been in Toulon for a couple of months, and Hal knew his way around. He took me up to the town and gave me hints on the best shops, and invited me aboard *Sentinel II*, where I spent the entire evening in her extremely cosy cabin. Supper was served on beautiful plates bought from "The China Shop" in Hamilton, well known to all visiting Americans. Inevitably we yarned until late about Bermuda and its people; I became quite nostalgic about it and wished I had never left there.

The next day I shopped in the morning, delighting in the variety and the more reasonable prices. For the first time in months I bought meat, a large and lean steak. After getting a good selection of vegetables I returned to the *Nova* for a feast. It was a great success; the steak proved tender and succulent, the vegetables cooked to a turn. When it was finished I lay down and slept.

Sprawling Toulon held no attraction for me apart from its cheapness. There are innumerable noisy water-front cafés, out of which came many drunks late at night. There always seemed to be a fight about to begin, but I rather think they wore themselves out shouting at each other. Shops, streets, cinemas and flats are very much the same in any large town, but Toulon had one redeeming feature, cheap opera in a gracious building in front of which played fountains.

One evening I saw an enormous coloured sailor arguing with two gendarmes. He was very drunk, and when I heard English being shouted with a Bronx accent I guessed that he was an American off one of the ships, so I thought I would try the Good Samaritan stunt. "Can I help you?" I asked cautiously. The sailor turned to me, draped an arm round my shoulder, and replied, "You can, these S.O.B.s pretend they can't understand me." He gazed belligerently at the two small gendarmes and then shouted at them, "I'm an American, you ———!" I told the police, who spoke no English, that I would see him to his ship; they looked relieved, saluted, and walked away. With the black colossus leaning heavily on me, I led the way to the quay. Passing the *Nova* I had the not so bright idea of giving the drunk some coffee, so with some difficulty I got him on board, and after bumping his head on most of the cabin beams got him seated on the bunk, and started to make the coffee. He stopped me doing this and brought out a flask. I took a swig— it was brandy. He drained the flask, leaned back and closed his eyes. "Oh lord," I thought, "he's going to sleep on me." I shook him violently and said I would take him back to his ship. Two glazed eyes looked at me for a moment, closed, opened again, and then he was violently sick. Feeling ill myself I got him ashore and then fortunately fell in with two more Americans. They took charge of him and I went back to clear up the mess—a most horrible job.

Hal and Winnie expressed a wish to come as far as Ciotat, and on 1st December I set off with them both on board. Light airs and calms prolonged the trip, but it was a warm, sunny day and they enjoyed it very much. When we arrived at our destination and tied up to the quay, the fact that Ciotat builds ships was impressed on us by the sound of many riveters at work, but it is a pleasant town with a good harbour. We had tea on the *Nova*, after which the Kitcheners returned by bus to Toulon.

I was held up in Ciotat four days, until a fierce mistral had blown itself out. On the second day the local paper reported that a gust of

250 kilometres (156¼ miles) per hour had been recorded by an observer on a hill near Marseilles. Hurricane force! The boat was very well sheltered, for the wind came off the land and in front of me was a row of tall houses, but I could sense the weight of the gale roaring overhead. It got colder and colder and this nearly caused my death. When night came I closed the hatch and lit the lamp and the pressure stove to warm up the cabin. After a while I felt very sleepy, and then I saw the lamp going out. My brain, working even more slowly than usual, sluggishly calculated how long ago the lamp had been filled. Oh yes, I had filled it on the previous night—it should last three days—why was it going out? Heavens! No oxygen! I staggered to the hatch, flung it open, and breathed in deeply from the cold pure air outside. On my return to the cabin the lamp was once more burning brightly! It was as good as a canary in a coal mine.

On 6th December the wind had moderated sufficiently for me to leave. I chose a narrow gap between a barren rocky island called Verte and the high cliffs of the mainland, one mile due south of Ciotat. It was a tricky piece of navigation, for I was able to tack right up to the base of the towering cliffs.

When two or three miles from Cassis Bay the wind dropped away, then returned half an hour later dead against me. I cursed, tried to beat against it, and then said, "Oh hell, I'll go to Cassis," and back I turned. With the wind astern the *Nova* glided along easily, but I had a tussle with my inner self, which kept on telling me I had gone soft and was afraid to leave the harbour. "All right, blast you," I told it, "I'll carry on to Marseilles," and there and then I turned back and headed westward once more. Drat the stricter inner man!

I drew level with the island of Rion, then Calseraigne, Jaise and Jarron, and finally Maire, the latter only a few hundred yards from the mainland. I had been told that an overhead cable had been taken across to the island, and it was doubtful whether I should get underneath with the mast up. I soon saw the cable sagging over the narrow strip of water, but there were yards to spare. With the island behind me I headed across the large bay towards Marseilles. The sun had set, the wind grew colder, and the spray seemed to freeze on my face. I stuck it as long as I could, but my teeth chattered together like a riveter's hammer, my hands and feet were painfully cold, and wind-tears ran from my eyes.

No longer able to stand this beating about in a choppy bay I headed the *Nova* towards an artificial harbour which had been built for pilot boats and lay between Ratonneau and Pomegues Islands.

I now made much better progress, not being so hard on the wind, and then for me there was a memorable happening. As I sailed past Chateau d'If Island I crossed the second of the three loops of the voyage, but the cold took all the thrill away.

Although I knew the *Nova* was sailing quite fast, it seemed an endless time before I actually got into the harbour. There were no public quays to moor up to here, and I tied up to the stern of a white motor-boat anchored in the centre.

By 10 o'clock next morning I left the island harbour, passed a few yards north of Chateau d'If Island, and made straight for Marseilles in a good fresh wind. Within an hour I was between the forts which, in olden days, guarded the entrance to the harbour. I lifted my eyes to the golden Madonna, high above the church on the hill, and felt she welcomed me back again.

20

WINTER IN FRANCE

I TIED up *Nova Espero* opposite the Town Hall, and although I did not know it then, I was destined to stay at Marseilles for a long time. When I visited Lloyd's agents to enquire about conditions on the waterways up country the new I gleaned was grim. I was told several of the waterways were frozen over and getting back up the Rhone might prove a difficult business, for unless I could find a barge with a captain who would tow me for the sake of a mere gratuity it might cost me anything up to £100 to get as far as Lyons.

So I had to make up my mind to stay in Marseilles for Christmas, and I relaxed both mentally and physically. To overcome the cold in the mornings I contrived breakfast in bed, by sitting in my bunk, twisting round to light the stove, then snuggling down into the blankets until the kettle boiled. When it did I twisted round again to make a pot of tea, and then replaced the kettle with a biscuit tin lid, containing several slices of bread. When the toast was ready I put it on my bunk and ate my breakfast, while immersed in a good book.

I did my careful shopping in the mornings, making do on two or three shillings a day. I found that a shilling's worth of minced beef scraps, when boiled with green split peas and potatoes, lasted me two days. For a time I was feeding an English-speaking Swiss, down on his uppers, at very little extra cost.

I was far from lonely, because I soon made many good friends in Marseilles. Among those who helped so much to make my stay a pleasant one were John and Mary Rayner, in charge of the blue Fairmile *May Queen*, a lawyer *Maitre*, who was extreme right in politics, and his doctor friend, Maurice, who was leftish, and Lionel Thomas, another acquaintance whom I met when I called at Lloyd's agents.

Christmas Day in Marseilles turned out to be one of the best I have ever had, although I had pangs of remorse at not being with my own family. The midday meal was taken aboard a smuggler's boat. He had recently been released from prison to return to his sweetheart and his right-hand man. He was busy as a beaver when I arrived, basting a chicken, checking the contents of various steaming pots, and drinking brandy. Later they all came aboard the *Nova* for tea, and in the evening I joined the party in the *May Queen*.

One morning I awoke feeling colder than usual. I seemed insulated from the world, for the city noise came through very muted. Daylight was reluctant to overcome the darkness, and I had to look at my chronometer to make sure it was time I had my morning cup of tea. When I finally emerged from my cocoon of blankets and tried to open the hatch I found it would not move. When I gave it an extra hard pull it came back with a rush, at the same time dislodging a large lump of something extremely cold, which fell on my face. Snow! A good nine inches of it covered the boat, and for a while the evening papers were full of pictures of this unusual South of France weather.

The days sped by, and still I stayed in harbour. The lowest price at which I was offered a tow was £30, far beyond my means, for my funds had now shrunk to a dangerous level. I had to break the law in order to eat. First I sold my sextant for eighteen pounds, and then my radio for ten pounds, hoping that if the customs displayed any curiosity they would believe that both articles had fallen overboard.

As untaxed petrol is not allowed for use on inland waterways I was about to break yet another law. I just could not afford to pay the land price for petrol, which worked out at three times the price of that of sea petrol. I scouted round and obtained all the cans and drums I could find, and then had them filled with customs free petrol. I stored all my illicit cargo in the forecastle, in the cockpit, and between the bunks. Enough for six hundred miles. I felt as though I had taken over the command of a tanker.

On 13th January I sailed out of Marseilles, very low in the water, with the intention of reaching Bouc in the Bay of Foss, or any port nearby before dark. It was a glistening day, with a biting north wind, but while the sun was near its meridian it was enjoyable. When it disappeared behind the darkening hills, the cold rapidly intensified, and I shrank further into my gaudy duffle coat, hoping to find a harbour before dark. By lucky chance I found myself opposite a port which could be none other than Sausset, about which I had been given information. Just in case the water was very shallow I lowered the sails, and entered slowly with the outboard, bringing up under a crane where I found four feet of water.

Frost formed on the inner surface of the cabin roof that night, but at 10 o'clock next morning I was on my way again with a fair wind behind me.

From Bouc, which was my next port of call, there is a little-used canal going up to Arles-sur-Rhone. I had thought that I would slip up there without too much attention from the customs, but I had no luck as I was stopped at the entrance of the canal, to get my triptyque endorsed for official entry into France. I heard the ominous words spoken by a superior to the man who boarded me, "Have you checked to see that the articles mentioned in the triptyque are on board?"

The man shook his head, and looked rather abashed. Accompanied this time by his superior, we all went to the *Nova*. The latter answered to her description, and the outboard number was checked and found correct. "Where is the radio? we must check that too."

"I, 'er; it's er; it's not here now."

"Oh!" said the chief, "no radio!" No sextant either, I said to myself. Aloud I replied, "It was no good to me." Then, to my great relief, he turned to the uniformed man and said, "Cross out the radio." Turning to me he said, "You have the sextant?"

"I'm afraid not." I answered. He looked at my harassed face and said, "All right, cross that off also." He smiled, shook me by the hand, and told me that I was free to proceed, and not to lose any more articles. What a relief!

This customs business and reporting to the police had taken three hours, and now the sun was setting. I started up the outboard and began moving along the Canal d'Arles à Bouc. By the time I had got under the first bridge, not without slight damage to the main truck of my mast, it was dark.

The canal stretched ahead of me like a river of pitch, straight as an arrow, its perspective point vanishing into the evening mist. I carried on for several hours, getting colder and colder, and finally stopped near a cluster of lighted houses, and after a simple supper of hot tea, bread and cheese I thankfully turned in.

When I awoke the next morning there was a strange crunching sound as I moved out of the bunk, and looking out of the hatch I saw that *Nova* had been frozen in. Fortunately it was thin ice, which broke at every motion of the boat. Nevertheless it was a disturbing state of affairs, for if this could happen so far south, what sort of conditions could I expect ahead?

However, a golden haze in the east announced the imminent arrival of the sun, and I had no doubt the ice would soon melt away. After breakfast I started, and all day I pushed on as fast as the outboard would go, sometimes grinding through ice, where the canal was shaded, and it remained frozen. There was an eerie kind of beauty along this canal. Tall reeds grew each side, where blue birds darted to and fro. Marshes and large stretches of water lay beyond the reeds. The sea shore puts in an appearance at one point, and for several miles you can hear the surf breaking on the beach.

Apart from the ice I had only one scare. Two-thirds of the way along the canal a small river enters on one side to keep up the level of the water, any surplus flowing out over a barred weir opposite. I did not notice that a tremendous amount of water was going over the fall, and was swept against the protecting bars with a disconcerting crash; once there, the pressure of the water held the boat tight. I got out of that predicament by scrambling along the top of the bars with a rope which I made fast to a tree just beyond the weir, then with the outboard flat out, and me hauling on the rope, the *Nova* scraped and bumped along each post until she was free.

As we drew near to Arles the reeds became thicker in places, leaving a passage only a few feet wide. Outside the town a railway bridge stopped me temporarily, and, when through I tied up alongside an old barge and strolled over to where the canal joined the River Rhone. I was shocked to see a huge sheet of ice lying in front of the lock, beyond which the river swirled its way to the sea. However, after various adventures and misadventures we succeeded in getting through, and a cheer broke out on the banks when I entered the calm waters inside the lock. The River Rhone which gets most of its water from the Alps was low, owing to the cold weather, and we descended at least twenty feet before we reached its level, and had the luck to moor for the night alongside a fellow countryman, another Fairmile named *Xrona* of Dartmouth.

Quadruple lock at Castelnaudary on the Canal du Midi

The "curtain" boat at Castelnaudary

The " Vieux Chateau" on Ile d' Yeu in the Bay of Biscay

Washing day on the inland waterways

I spent many days at Arles trying to get a tow up to Lyons. The charges were prohibitive, and in some cases ridiculous. Twice I attempted to get up under my own power, but each time my efforts only served to prove that it could not be done by the outboard, even when helped by sails.

One afternoon I was cleaning up the boat when a group of men rushed to the side of the quay, climbed down to Ashworth's *Xrona* and crossed over to the side where I was. They were extremely excited and pointed to the river. They spoke so rapidly that I could not understand a word they said, and told them so. Then they started using signs, and I gathered that one of them had lost his hat when crossing a bridge higher up the river. I beckoned them to come on board and rather leisurely set off for mid-stream. Once there I spied something floating in the water and made for it; to my horror I saw that it was the body of an elderly man. My two companions fished for him with an oar and missed him, and then after I had circled round again they got him at their second attempt. I motored over to an empty barge on which there were several men standing, and got them to help to lift the body on to the barge. To my surprise two men in white coats hurried along and started artificial respiration. Later that day I managed to get the story. The old man had jumped off the bridge bent on suicide. What upset me was that I could have been quicker if I had known what it was all about; perhaps we could have been in time to bring the old fellow back to life. How much easier it would be if all nations had a common language.

At last I realized I would never get up the Rhone, and would have to make up my mind to return to the Mediterranean. Instead of retracing my steps along the canal back to Bouc, it would be quicker to go down the River Rhone to Port St. Louis. I had no chart of these parts or of the coast, when I should arrive there, but luckily I met a pilot who drew a sketch map for me. It was March when I finally tore myself away from the *Xrona*'s side to venture down the swirling, moody river I had grown to hate.

With my five knots, and the river's four or five knots (it flows at ten or twelve kilometres an hour higher up), the banks whizzed past with unaccustomed rapidity, but I got no pleasure from it; I felt tense and apprehensive, and the water boiling over the shallows did not help

K

matters. The pencil chart which a pilot had drawn for me was a great asset, for it told me on which side of the river to keep, and by watching the kilometre sign posts on the bank I knew when to change over. The pilot had warned me of one particularly tricky bit—the rest was easy according to him. The stretch of river he mentioned approached and my apprehension mounted when I could see nothing of the essential kilometre sign, but I made out a house that he had told me was near the danger point. I knew I had to cross soon to the right bank, a case of "must," for apart from a narrow channel the river ran rapidly over a ledge. Not knowing exactly where I was, I left the swing to the right too late, and saw a line of broken water right ahead. Quickly I turned the *Nova* round and she just managed to hold her own against the current. Slowly I edged over towards the other bank, hoping the outboard would not let me down, but it kept on purring away until I was in the deeper water of the channel; then, by easing down the motor, I edged past that nasty section of the river without mishap.

The rest of the way was easy going. The Rhone slowed down to a crawl and I relaxed and enjoyed myself. The sun was brilliant in a cloudless sky and, for a change, no cold wind was whistling over the flat country. All was peaceful. Stark against the sky loomed the buildings of Port St. Louis, its quay lined with barges. At Port St. Louis it is necessary to leave the river and enter a lock leading to a mile-long canal which leads to the Bay of Foss, because the Rhone enters the Mediterranean over a shallow bar with less than three feet of water above it.

I negotiated the lock after narrowly escaping collision with a bridge which was lowered almost in my face. Next morning I was up at 6.30 a.m., and got under way shortly after, going first to the east along the cut, then south down the Bay of Foss, and finally heading west towards the Gulf du Lion, a place notorious for its sudden fierce storms.

The wind was light and my progress slow, but it was a clear sunny day and I had many fishing-boats around for company. The water from the Rhone came swirling out to sea for about a mile, making a sharp contrast in colour to the Mediterranean. I followed the coast for about twenty miles; It was low-lying and desolate with everlasting sand-dunes which, in places, cut off the sea from vast salt lakes. Nothing grows there but stunted shrubs and coarse sand-grass. At the end of the twenty miles of coastal sailing I laid a course directly across the gulf to Cette, thirty miles away. The north-west wind increased in strength as soon as I cleared away from the land, so I fastened the sheets, lashed the tiller and let the *Nova* sail herself. In two hours all sight of land disappeared and I had the sea to myself, for I had left the fishing grounds behind.

The everlasting rising and falling motion of the *Nova* had a soporific effect on me after so much time in smooth water, and sitting in the cockpit, I dozed in the sun. Darkness came before I sighted land, though shortly after I saw two orange coloured lights far away in the distance. Knowing that Cette had an oil refinery, I guessed that the lights I saw were caused by burning waste gases like those at the new refinery near Southampton.

Midnight chimes heralded my entrance into Cette, cold and tired. With the outboard ticking over slowly I wandered up several off-shoots of the port before I found an excellent berth near a couple of yachts. The place was a miniature Venice; I discovered later that there are eight kilometres of waterways running through the town.

The first day I did a little exploring and some shopping, and decided I liked the place. There I met a Monsieur Le Quellec and his son, who had had a new boat built in Normandy, and was expecting her arrival the next day. As promised the new boat arrived next afternoon, and I witnessed her launching.

Walking down the quay one day I saw a sight that would have gladdened the heart of any wine-bibber. A ship, looking exactly like an oil-tanker, was discharging her cargo—wine! A line of motor-lorries, similar to our own petrol-lorries, was drawn up by the ship, and to each one was a length of hose-pipe; still more hoses wandered across the street to wine-cellars. Some dripped at the joints making purple puddles, and filling the air with vinous perfume. The bad leaks all had a beaker underneath and I just could not resist dipping my finger in one for a taste. Ugh! It was strong and sour. I described the sight I had seen to M. Le Quellec, and he told me that the ship was one of several belonging to him. He told me also that he shipped quantities of cider to a large manufacturer in England. I was surprised to hear this, knowing how many tons of apples are wasted every year in this country.

I decided to go to Spain before returning to England. For one thing it was very close, and for another I had two friends in Barcelona. I wrote to England for charts, but they took so long to arrive, and I received so many letters urging me to return home, that I gave up the idea.

On 5th April I filled up my only empty petrol can, without having to answer any damning questions from the customs. I decided not to enter the Canal au Midi from Cette, but to sail south to Agde as though I were really going to Spain, and try to get into the canal from there, though I had been warned that the connecting branch had not been used for years and it might be silted up.

On 7th April, after ten days in Cette, a very dry Cette, for they had not had any rain for months, to the great concern of the farmers, I hoisted my sails to a light head wind, and started beating down to Agde to enter a new phase of the journey.

21

THE CANAL DU MIDI

THE TOWN of Agde lies about two miles inland, but a river has been widened and deepened to give easy access to the sea. Near the entrance I was hailed by the customs to stop and come to the quay. "Now for it," I thought, as I came alongside their motor-boat. Before I could get out the hatchway was darkened by the body of a man climbing inside. A very large man with a face like a bulldog struggled in and sat on the other bunk.

I immediately offered him a cup of tea and a cigarette; at the mention of the last word he said, "How many cigarettes do you have?" and waved aside the proffered tin. He licked the stub of a pencil and laboriously wrote the number I gave him in a note book. He asked many questions, including the number of the outboard, but no mention of petrol. After he had got down everything he wanted he relaxed, smiled, and said, "Now, why does a man sail about all by himself?"

"It is very simple," I replied. "If you have a male companion it is impossible, unless you are very fortunate, to agree *all* the time; and if you have a female companion there will be strife all the way. I'm just a selfish man who likes to please himself." As he was climbing out he asked the dreaded question, "How much petrol do you carry?" to which I replied, "My outboard takes very little for it is only four horse-power." This evasive answer satisfied him, and he wished me *Bon Voyage* before I left for Agde.

The town was an old place with many fishing-boats tied up alongside, and dingy cafes lining the street near the water-front. I walked along the bank to see where the entrance to the Midi was made. My heart sank when I saw a narrow weedy-looking channel cut from the river to the canal. It was about five hundred yards long, and ended in some lock-gates that looked as though they had not been opened for centuries.

The best thing to do, I thought, would be to have a word with the lock-keeper. When I reached the house I asked a woman who was busy scrubbing a table outside if I might speak to the "man of the lock." She screeched a name once or twice and a man came ambling out. I asked him whether it would be possible for me to bring a boat up and enter the canal. He scratched his head, looked very doubtful, and then asked me how much water my boat drew. When I replied that it was only a metre he announced that I might just do it, but he was uncertain about the possibility of opening the gates. I put a hundred francs in his hand and said, "Perhaps you will try?" "Bring up your boat—if you can, and I will," he answered, and went back indoors.

I had some trouble getting under a wooden footbridge, and it was dark before I got things sorted out, but by the light of a street lamp I could see the lock-keeper trying to open the gates. With the keel of the *Nova* pushing through soft ooze I went right up to where he was working. I heard him call out to someone, and a second man came out to give him a hand, and then another. With three men straining away on the handles something was bound to happen. Many creaks and groans began to come from the gates, and one slowly opened, the other was easy, and soon I was in a circular lock on the Canal du Midi. The gates were closed where I had just entered, the sluice-gates opened, the *Nova* rose five feet, and then I went through the gates opposite and moored alongside a quay a few yards from the lock. I walked back and gave the keeper and his helpers some cigars, and after cooking a meal turned in well satisfied with the day.

I set off early next morning along the canal listening carefully to the motor. I realized that it had a tremendous task ahead of it, and, at this stage, was not sure whether it would be strong enough for the job. The first three locks I reached were all operated by very old women. Each was pleasant and seemed highly amused to be given Turkish cigarettes. In quick succession came two double locks giving me a lift of twenty feet each time. Controlling the *Nova* in these was not an easy task, and it brought home to me the fact that at times a companion would be useful. I passed a village, turned a corner, and saw that the canal had widened out, and was now lined with dark green conifers. They made a lovely picture as they ended in a letter "V" against the clear sky in the distance, with the reflection in the water reversing the image.

At the end of the green avenue I turned another corner and saw an awe-inspiring sight. Six locks, one above the other, climbed up the side of a steep hill, with foaming water shooting from one to the other. I moored alongside the bank to watch a couple of barges being taken up. They were making easy work of it, for they had steel cables out ahead, and they were too big to be tossed about by the swirling, foaming water. The more I watched the less I liked the idea of taking the *Nova* up, but of course there was no alternative.

These locks are electrically operated, which means that all four sluice gates are opened at once, hence the tremendous influx of water into the "empties." I climbed up to the control tower and explained to the man in charge that I wished to take up a small wooden boat, and that I was on my own. When I had finished my plea I handed him a cigar. He called to a man standing by and told him to help me through; then, turning back to me, said, "For you I will let the water in very, very slowly." I went back to the *Nova* feeling lighter in heart and stood by waiting for my turn.

As is usual in such cases, the actual performance was not so bad as the anticipation. The big rubber tyres I had picked up cushioned the bumps most effectively.

It was a day full of interest for, apart from my introduction to multiple locks, the canal was aqueducted over rivers way below, past quiet rustic villages, and between avenues of majestic trees whose branches met overhead like a timber Gothic cathedral.

My spirits were damped the following day, for it poured hard from dawn to dusk. However, I did get a great deal of satisfaction from the unfailing efforts of the outboard, which took the continuous downpour without a cough or sneeze. It was running twelve hours without a break, for even in the locks I kept it ticking over.

It was still raining when I awoke the next day, but I carried on with the firm determination not to dally any more. All along this lovely stretch of the route I got kindness and help from the lock-keepers. In order to have quiet nights I usually tied up to the bank on some lonely stretch of water. Here, in glorious solitude where the only noises in the night were the cry of a night bird or the croaking of a frog, I read by the cabin lamp with the hatch wide open, completely content.

The days passed by with every one full of new sights and scenery. A glimpse of the snow-capped Pyrenees dividing France from Spain, women kneeling in wooden boxes at the canal-side doing their laundry, regardless of the bloated bodies of drowned kittens and puppies, which were numerous near the towns. The trees, always a source of admiration for me, were heralding the spring. The pale green of new leaves, emerging from their light russet-coloured buds, filled the air underneath the arching branches overhead with green and golden sunbeams. On either side stretched the interminable vineyards, with the gnarled stunted vines only just beginning to show signs of life. The red-brown soil was weedless and furrowed to absorb the water.

The sun had just risen above the horizon on 11th April, and I was having my breakfast looking forward to another good day's run, when a small pebble rattled on the cabin-top. I looked up through the hatch and saw a man standing on the towpath with a bicycle. He shouted, "Get moving, the water is going to be let out of the canal." I could not understand what he was saying at first and the poor chap had to repeat his message three times. "When will they do this?" I asked. "Tomorrow night, hurry on immediately to Carcassonne." I quickly finished my spoilt breakfast, entered in my diary, "What next? They are going to let the water out of the bloody canal," and set off.

When I reached Carcassonne in the late afternoon and looked down upon it, for the canal ran round the side of a hill above, I thought it would be an interesting place to stay for a few days, not only for the sake of its romantic looking turrets, towers, and high walls—a camera-carrying tourist's Mecca—but because its principal architect was a namesake of mine—the Duc de Violet.

When I reached the town quays I saw my barges tying up, and squeezed in between a couple to the bank so that I could get ashore easily. Just ahead was a large lock. Many children gathered round to stare at the *Nova*, and I asked one of them if he knew how long the canal would be closed. I do not think he really understood me, but he ran away and came back with a man in a peaked cap. When I asked him the same question he also failed to understand my French, but with that wonderful courtesy shown by most people of France he went away for a young man who spoke a few words of English, and when he arrived I learned that it would be two weeks. He also informed me that the local workmen spoke a patois very difficult for a foreigner to understand, and then I remembered an awful *faux pas* I had committed at one lock. When I heard the lock-keeper say "*una*" for "one" I asked him whether he was Italian. Most indignant he was.

I was told that I could push on as far as Castelnaudary if I wished, and that the necessary arrangements would be made. Thinking of the very few francs I had left, I decided to carry on as far as possible. The locks usually close at 7 p.m., but that night, advised by phone from Carcassonne, they remained open later especially for me. It was a pitch-black night, and I had difficulty in following the curves of the canal, but when I reached the locks there was always a man or woman with a torch to guide me in. I was amazed at the kindness and consideration shown. At one lock I handed over my permits, and, unknown to me, all my slender store of francs had got into the folds. It was all handed back to me with a smile, and a warning to be more careful. By midnight I had had all I could take, and the outboard had been running for seventeen hours; both of us, I decided, needed a rest. Having reached a lock, I passed through, and then told the keeper that I was stopping for sleep.

By 6 a.m. we were on our way again, reaching Castelnaudary in the afternoon and there, after climbing up a "bank" of four electrically operated locks, I moored in a large pool which I was told would not be emptied. I felt very low in spirits at the thought that I would be captive there for fourteen days, but the time passed more quickly than I expected. The *Nova* had more attention than she had received for a long time; the cabin sides were scraped down to the bare wood and three coats of varnish put on. I would have painted her dirty- scarred sides if I had been able to afford the paint; as it was I heard a party of schoolgirls, escorted by a nun, exclaim "*Ooh, jolie*," as they pointed to the boat when passing over the bridge just ahead. The local children got into the habit of standing on the same bridge and shouting, "Are you English?" and keeping it up until I answered, "Yes, I am."

I learned something else amusing—if a child said or did anything foolish he or she would be called "*Anglais*"—a great insult!

I found out, to my own satisfaction if to nobody else's, that the mistral starts in Castelnaudary, not the Rhone as the experts believe. Nearly every day the wind blew fierce and cold.

What gave me the greatest pleasure in Castelnaudary were the nightingales. Just before midnight I would go for a walk along a country road where the trees and fields were bathed in the pale light of the moon, and listen to their clear sweet song. By walking quietly I could get within a few feet of one songster. High up in a tall tree, whose intricate branches looked like black lace against the starry sky, sat a lonely bird who, to my intense amusement, in the midst of all the glorious chorus from nightingales near and far, could only manage a single raucous "honk" every half minute.

On market days the town came to life; all the farmers and their wives came riding in, usually by horse and cart. Stalls circled the square, selling all kinds of food and sweets, or cheap, shoddy clothing. Agricultural implements would line the pavements, each surrounded by a group of farmers discussing its merits and demerits. Most were American or Canadian, although I did see a few Ferguson tractors. There is every sign that the French peasant is becoming increasingly mechanically minded.

I finally got away on 28th April, in the middle of a thunderstorm, but I only made about fifteen miles, for the rain was heavy enough to keep me below most of the time. By starting extra early on the following morning, however, I managed to reach Toulouse by evening. I had grim warnings that a large town was near by the unpleasant yellowish-brown water, and by the increasing number of corpses around. Contrary to popular belief, it is only near towns and villages that the canal is foul, elsewhere the water is quite clean. Just before Toulouse I reached the highest point on this, the oldest and first large canal in France. It was built in the sixteen-hundreds, and the engineer who built it received so many rebuffs and such lack of co-operation that he broke his heart, and died before it was complete; but an admirer built a monument to him on the highest point. A gigantic task had faced him; the Garonne had to be crossed several times, and there were many hills to be climbed. The canal still remains a noteworthy feat of French engineering, with its stonework in excellent condition.

Toulouse, a large rambling nondescript city, held nothing of interest to me, and as I passed the endless lines of barges tied up to the quays I had no doubt that my stay would be short.

22

TOULOUSE TO BORDEAUX

WITHIN TWENTY hours I was on my way again with a good supply
of food from the Monoprix, the cheapest place to buy food in France,
although always very crowded. A double lock, a short straight run,
under a bridge, and then I was lost on a sheet of water almost surrounded by a high wall, arched in several places where canals entered
the pool. It was like a railway terminus without any signs or signals,
and I had to seek directions to find which was the right arch.

The canal now ran in dead straight stretches many miles in length,
and here no tall trees lined the banks. In the evening I moved inshore
through the reeds and tied up to a tree. The bright yellow heads of
water-irises swayed above the after-deck.

Bright and early I started the outboard buzzing, and as I had one of
the inevitable locks to negotiate I blew my foghorn loud and lustily,
like a posthorn on an eighteenth century stage-coach. There was no
response; I blew with greater force but still no one emerged from the
keeper's cottage. I stopped nearby, got ashore, and walked up to the
building. The door was open, and inside sitting at a table drinking wine
was a small rotund middle-aged man, neatly dressed in navy blue.
"Can you open the lock, if you please?" I asked. "No, not today, it is
the fête," he replied, looking very indignant at such an unreasonable
request. Then I remembered that it was the glorious 1st of May, when
Moscow and her satellites proclaim the unity of the workers, and the
English dance round maypoles, weather permitting.

Away in the distance I could see a church spire pointing up above
some trees. By choosing a path in that direction I eventually came to a
pleasant village, its houses clustered round the church. I sat on a seat
in the square and watched the people. They were like one big happy
family, for they all seemed to be on most friendly terms with one
another; perhaps it was the fête. The old boy from the lock paid me a

visit in the evening. He was a red-hot Communist and an ex-Navy man; he treated me to a long harangue about the time when everything would belong to the people who did the work, and he looked forward to the time when Europe joined up with Russia and faced that stronghold of capitalism, America, with complete unity.

May 2nd was an excellent day's run, and I passed through the thirty-first lock from Toulouse before closing time on the canal. It was surprising how much interest and amusement the *Nova* caused as she passed through the villages with the outboard buzzing like an angry wasp. Children ran along the towpath or rode bicycles to keep company with me, women called to their husbands to come and have a look, and all sorts of questions were fired at me when I was held stationary in the locks. The canal had now regained its old beauty; the trees, their trunks mottled with yellow, green and brown, once again lined the banks, and were becoming more leafy. Around the keepers' cottages usually twined a purple haze of wisteria, called by them *glycein*. Along the canal-edge grew the yellow irises and delicate white flowers that looked like enormous snowdrops.

For the next three days I continued at a good pace, and on long stretches between locks I amused myself by singing in harmony (?) with the single note of the engine, making chords and discords with it and improving my own version of well-known songs.

Out of all the people I met operating the locks, to whom I usually gave cigarettes, only one ever asked me for anything. In this particular case the lock-keeper was an old witch-like woman with a game leg. After I had given her the usual gratuity of cigarettes she asked for English chocolate. I explained that I had been away from England for more than a year, whereupon she requested tinned food, then money. I told her that I had no tinned food and very little money, but she said, "All Englishmen are rich, you just won't give anything to a poor old woman." As I left the lock she called out, "I hate the English and you are a mean animal." At least, that was the best I could translate.

On a warm sunny afternoon, the 5th of May, I arrived at Castets, where the canal ends and you are dropped by lock to the river Garonne, thirty miles from Bordeaux. Major Kitchener had written to a friend of his in Bordeaux, a Colonel Pucheu, telling him that I might pass that way.

I moored up near the lock, for I had no intention of descending the Garonne without plenty of daylight in hand.

At noon next day I entered the lock, and was lowered down until the top of the mainmast, which I had raised while waiting, was level with the stonework. The strength of the current fooled me as I was leaving, and pushed me up against a wall with a vicious bump.

About half a mile ahead a barge was also going down river, and I opened the outboard flat out to try to keep up with her, changing to the left or right bank when she did. Unfortunately I lost sight of her when refilling the petrol tank, and had to guess the rest.

Along one section of the river I ran into an imitation snow storm. Downlike seeds from a wood were being blown across the river by a strong wind. The volume was incredible, billions of them, and I am still finding signs of them in odd crevices on the boat. I gazed at the blue sky above and pondered over the question of just how high some of them would get. I remembered reading somewhere that tiny spiders in sails of web had been found at fifteen thousand feet, and small flies and other winged insects could be found anywhere from three to ten thousand feet. I had no doubt some of these seeds would reach terrific heights and travel hundreds of miles.

I passed under a railway bridge while a train roared overhead, and entered a sphere of great activity. Ships, barges and motor-boats were moving about with purposeful activity. After tying up to a barge on which lived an old couple, retired from active service like their vessel, I asked the old lady where I could get some water. "Oh monsieur, it is too late. The tap is already turned off, but I will give you some," she said. I passed her my bottle, and while I was waiting her husband told me to put out extra mooring-ropes, for the tide was very fierce. I was glad he warned me, for when the tide began flowing up I noticed that my stern line was bar-taut.

Going up to the town to hunt for some bread, I fell in with three men from whom I enquired the way to the nearest *boulangerie*. They insisted on taking me to a café for aperitifs; alas, I had too many, and when negotiating the gangplank to the barge I stumbled, and the loaf disappeared into the brown flood. The dear old lady came to my rescue again, sold me half a loaf, and made a crack about drinking wine on an empty stomach.

In the morning I awoke with a nasty headache, but managed to ring Colonel Pucheu after soliciting help from a bartender. His daughter, who had journeyed to the Mediterranean with the Kitcheners, answered the phone, and thank goodness she spoke excellent English. She invited me to come down to their flat right away, and gave me careful instructions on how to get there.

At lunch the colonel was very amused by my pronunciation of certain French words like *rue*, Pucheu and *mareu*; the last one he told me was French for a baby cod, and one he always used to ask me to pronounce when we were in company. I found out later that it also meant a woman of easy virtue.

Such was the kindness of the Pucheu family that I stayed much longer than I felt I should, and did not tear myself away until the 14th of May, when a fresh south-easterly breeze was blowing to help me on my way. It was nice to be able to use the sails once more.

I had the tide with me until I was five miles past Blaye, then the wind lightened and, as I had taken the wrong channel, going to the north-hand side of a group of islands instead of to the south, I anchored. By sounding with my boathook I discovered that there was six feet of water beneath the boat. In the next hour grey humps of mud banks rose out of the lowering water, and at dead low tide I found myself in a puddle three feet deep, amid vast stretches of mud. It was high tide at 8 p.m. So in the darkness with a rising wind I set sail again over the banks, sounding all the time with my boathook, and at 10 o'clock I anchored again, this time near the port-hand channel. It was a miserable night, with wind and tide struggling against each other for the control of the *Nova*. Steamers passed frequently, making a wash which rattled me inside the *Nova* like a pea in a pod.

The water began its race to the sea, and at 9 o'clock next morning I thankfully went with it. At midday the wind suddenly began to blow hard from the south-west. The *Nova* kicked up her heels, lay over on her side, and surged forward with a new lease of life, such as she had not shown for many months. The river was five or six miles wide now, and a short chop appeared almost at once, making the spray from the *Nova* fly high in the air. All very exhilarating.

Where the river enters the Bay of Biscay there are two ports, the one on the northern side is Royan, which dries out at low tide, that on the south is a very small harbour called Port Bloc, which stays navigable all round the clock. As I was passing Port Bloc I saw the southerly gale cone hoisted at the signal station. Thinking that discretion was the better part of valour, I turned into the harbour.

It was difficult to find a berth, for the quay on the left was built on piles twenty feet above the water—it was now low tide. On my right was the ferry slip where boats from Royan came frequently, and dead ahead was a steep slope of sand. In the end, after circling round several times, I tied up to a long white motor-boat so that at least I would not have to worry about the rise and fall of the tide.

There were only a few isolated houses round the port; the village, I learned, was a couple of miles away. Within a stone's throw of the sandy beach opposite were hundreds of thorny acacias, all in flower, and that night I fell asleep with their exotic perfume in my nostrils, and in my ears the distant roar of the Atlantic rollers falling on the beaches beyond Point de Grave.

23

HEADWINDS IN THE BAY OF BISCAY

THE GALE warning was still flying from its staff next morning. That and the lure of perfumed woods made it easy to decide to stay. After breakfast I walked through the acacia woods until I came to the sand-dunes bordering the beaches. On top of them, every hundred yards or so, were heavily fortified gun-emplacements, now derelict and useless; evidently they had been subjected to fierce bombardment before the end of the war, for they were deeply scarred and some had gaping cracks in their ten feet thick walls. Inside each were printed notices in German. The sun was warm as I wandered along the beach where the big rollers thundered continuously. Far out to sea was a lonely light-house built on a submerged reef. Even from where I stood I could see the white gleam of surf round its base. I turned my gaze back to the grey concrete ruins of the gun-emplacements, and thought that here was a typical paradox of human endeavour; one side so wise, useful and life-saving, the other designed only for blood and death. After a paddle in the cool pools left by the tide I left the beach and went back into the wood. In a clearing by a dusty lane was a graveyard. I counted a hundred wooden crosses each bearing a German name, except a few which said "Unknown." One or two had a withered bunch of flowers on top.

As chance would have it I witnessed a piece of revolting cruelty when I got back to the quay. A man in charge of a gravel-grading plant showed me five or six mice he had caught in a wire cage. I said to him, "What are you going to do with them? Turn them loose or drown them?" He shook his head and smiled. I turned away to the customs man to ask him about getting some petrol. He said that he would be issuing petrol to the fishermen the next day, and if I brought my cans along then they would be filled. Just as I turned round again I saw a man set fire to a small pool of petrol, in the centre of which stood the cage of mice. Horrified I saw the little creatures frantically try to escape and then succumb. I strode in a rage to the group watching their "play," and told them that I thought it was a beastly thing to do, and that in some countries their action would mean a fine, or even imprisonment. They merely laughed, shrugged their shoulders, and said that mice stole food. I suppose people have to be educated to the fact that animals have nerves and feel pain as we humans do.

Fierce thunderstorms disturbed the night, but in the morning there was not a breath of wind, so the weather was useless for me, especially as I was going into an area of strong coastal currents. On 18th May it rained all day, and on the 19th there was again no wind, but on the 20th at 9 o'clock I left my snug harbour and headed out into the Bay. Once clear of the Gironde and we were sailing up and down on a nicely rounded swell. The fun of sailing on such a day and in such conditions is hard to beat. With the wind astern, and the spinnaker ballooning out ahead, the *Nova* entered into the spirit of the day and tore along over the blue seas with a white bone in her teeth.

All good things come to an end; half way along the western side of Ile d'Oleron the wind dropped and we were left rolling in the swell. An hour later we got on the move again with a light north-westerly, but this meant continuous tacking and the long low island seemed interminable. Towards the northern tip rocky shoals reached out into the ocean, and I had to alter course further seawards. As the sun was sinking I at last rounded the northern tip, where stood a graceful black and white light tower. Then, with the wind on my beam, I sped as straight as an arrow for La Rochelle. Although it was dark before I reached the long dredged channel leading to the port, I had no difficulty, for the leading lights were excellent; by just keeping them one above the other I sailed confidently in, past two mediaeval towers guarding the entrance, and tied up to a fishing-boat, of which there were many of about sixty feet long.

Next morning the skipper, a young man full of energy, and half-owner of his craft—the *Gilbert Andre*—took me ashore. The town was old and crowded. In bygone days, before La Pallice was built, it was a harbour of great importance. There are many houses and buildings of interest to see but I was not given any time, being led from one café to the next. On the way back to our respective boats, a hazy walk for me, the skipper said, "You must eat with us to see what we fishermen

L

live on." I climbed down the vertical ladder with the others, and was seated on a bunk, swept clear of crumbs for my benefit. First of all bottles of wine were placed on the table, and we had a long drink; then the "mouse" (ship's boy) brought in a large crusty loaf, about a couple of pounds of butter, a bucket of oysters, a pot of lobsters and a dish of radishes. A man next to me opened up the oysters with his sheaf-knife, and handed them to me, but a dozen were all I could manage; then the skipper picked a fine lobster, broke it in two, and passed me the flaky tail part. I helped this down with radishes and strong Algerian wine, throwing the debris into a tin on the cabin floor.

In the middle of this orgy two yachtsmen cautiously descended the ladder. They had come to pay a courtesy call on me, found no one in the *Nova*, and guessed that I might be aboard the fishing-boat. One was M. Fernand Hervé, secretary of the Societe des Regates Rochelaise, and the other a well-known yachtsman from Bordeaux. Although refusing to eat they joined us in wine. It was a jolly party, and did not break up until 4 p.m. By this time the skipper was very drunk, and I, alas, was sick.

The *Gilbert Andre* got ready to sail at 10 p.m. After fond farewells and winey kisses on both cheeks I drew back the *Nova* alongside another boat, and stood by to watch the skipper, who by this time could hardly stand, take out his craft. I feared for his boat, for he left his berth at full speed, crashed into the boat ahead, carried on regardless of angry cries which followed him, lifted his boat up several inches when running over a mud bank on the other side of the harbour—with only the powerful diesel pushing him through that trouble—and finally missed the entrance and had to have a second shot at it. When his stern light disappeared from view I wondered how he would feel in the early hours of the morning.

One of the last things the skipper had said to me was, "Make for Ile d'Yeu, it's my home, and we may be there if all goes well." Going down below to sleep I decided to do as he suggested. At 8.30 the next morning I passed between the two towers and down the channel. Against the north-west wind I tacked past the tall quays of La Pallice, and the Ile de Ré.

All day long I tacked against the pestilential north-westerly and over broken seas that ran on the back of the ocean swell. Long after dark

I was still plugging back and forth without making much progress towards Ile d'Yeu. The lights of the Sables tempted me and I fell for the peace and quiet they offered. By midnight I had entered the long narrow first port, turned into a smoother part at the top, and tied up alongside a police boat, on which I noticed next morning a notice which read, "Do not moor alongside." Thank goodness I had put out extra fenders. The two police who boarded me laughed when I apologized for disregarding the notice, and said, "It does not count for you, monsieur, you cannot read French."

After getting bread and water I set off once more for Port Breton on Ile d'Yeu. Waiting outside was the wind, still dead against me. It was fun, while the sun shone, but by nightfall the island was still a long distance away, and my eyes felt tired. The flashing red light on Point de Corbeau, on the south of the island, slowly became clearer, and then I was working in smoother water in the lee of the dark shadowy land. Carefully following the leading lights I entered the deserted outer harbour of Port Breton and tied up to a solitary buoy. It was half an hour past midnight and I was all in, for I had not really recovered my health after my illness in North Africa.

I awoke late to the sound of shouting. Standing on the quay was a group of fishermen waving to me; they were my friends from La Rochelle. To get ashore I sailed over to some stone steps, left the *Nova* tied there, and walked round to the crew of the *Gilbert Andre*. They had had the bad luck of losing their trawl, and were now busy splicing up a new wire. The skipper invited me to his cottage to meet his wife and children, and also to join him in the midday meal.

In order to see something of the island I borrowed the skipper's bicycle, and one-legged it over the rutty road towards the western side where, I was told, an eleventh century castle could be found. I followed the direction indicated by several signposts bearing the legend "*vieux chateau*," and I eventually reached the castle, a masterpiece of mediaeval "home defence," built on precipitous rocks and surrounded by water at high tide. A drawbridge, now fixed permanently down, connected it to the mainland. It was in a remarkable state of preservation, being built of exceptionally hard stone. I climbed its ramparts and descended its dungeons, then sat in the shade of a rock further out to sea, and ruminated on how life must have been in days long ago in such

a castle in such a place. The island had once belonged to England and
once to Spain, so there was plenty of scope for the imagination.

I walked slowly back across the hummocky field to where I had left
the bicycle in the pathway. After gathering a bunch of honeysuckle for
the *Nova*'s cabin, I cycled back to Port Breton, where I left my
seat-biting steed outside a café in accordance with the skipper's
instructions.

On 27th May I set off once more against the familiar north-west
wind. Soon after the sun rose above the horizon. A rough confused sea
had been left by bad weather on the previous day and the going was
hard, but the tide was in my favour. By midday I could see the gap
between the dreaded Ile de Noirmoutier and the mainland. Fourteen
miles due west of the gap a buoy was marked on the chart, and I had to
find it so that I could lay a course to clear a nasty mess of rocks, reefs
and shoals known as Les Boeufs. I never did find the buoy, but instead
found myself in among Les Boeufs. Some were marked with a staff and
coloured, but I could find none that agreed with those on the chart.
It is a bad spot to be in when you know your position exactly, and a
frightening one when you don't. The broken sea around me was just
the sort the *Nova* did not like, and as I headed west she seemed reluctant
to leave the place. The strain of being on the alert for a grinding crash
was awful, and I wished I had stayed in Port Breton and waited for a
favourable wind. To the north-west of Noirmoutier lies a humped
backed rock called Ile du Pilier, with a prominent lighthouse on top of
it. Suddenly I spotted it, and at last I was able to make a rough fix of my
position. I decided to go through the narrow channel which lies
between the rock and Noirmoutier. Keeping my eyes open for any
extra light-coloured patches of water, for there are banks with only
eighteen inches of water above them at low water springs, I headed
north-east on a course for St. Nazaire. Since midday the wind had
steadily risen, and half way between the island and the mainland I was
down to jib and mizen, taking bucketsful of spray over me every few
seconds. As it looked as though I would not be able to clear a point of
land ahead (Point de St. Gildas) I turned and ran with the gale on my
stern down the hazard-strewn Bay de Bourgneuf. Six miles from Point
de St. Gildas to the east lay a tiny port called Pornic. It had the dis-
advantage of drying out completely at low water, but I hoped there

would be enough water when I arrived to let me get inside and tie up to something solid.

The town of Pornic lies at the top of a three-quarter-mile long inlet. Having reset a reefed mainsail I tore up the smooth water of the channel at a breakneck speed. Near the top some men shouted to me saying, "Too fast, take down your sail." Thinking there was very little water ahead I lowered all three sails in record time, and *Nova* glided to a thankful full stop alongside a quay. What a day!

While I was regaining my self-esteem with a cup of tea a man and his daughter, a dark-haired beauty, came to where the boat was lying and asked me where I had come from. When I said, "Ile d'Yeu," the man exclaimed, "Wasn't it very windy? I took my sailboat out earlier on but it got too bad and I soon came back." This remark fully restored my self-esteem, and I invited them both to join me for tea.

Up at 4.45 next morning to catch the tide I began a very early struggle against the wind, covering the ground lost the day before, and I eventually reached St. Nazaire's tall quays (twenty-foot tides) in the afternoon. The town, newly built since the war, was dull and character-less. The quays beyond the lock-gates were very busy: many ships, large and small, were loading or discharging. The notorious submarine pens, although scarred in places, still looked usable, and undoubtedly they will stand for many years as examples of heavy concrete construction.

Again keeping early hours I left St. Nazaire at 5 a.m. bound for Le Croisic. This famous fishing-port is built on the southern side of a great tidal lake, but dries out, like Pornic, at low water. Within a few hours of arriving there I was able to walk on the bottom, strewn with rotting crabs and lobsters. I inspected the *Nova* and was very glad to see she had very little weed on her.

For the next two days the wind blew with great strength. The fishermen stayed in port, and I felt justified in doing likewise.

24

THE BEAUTIFUL VILAINE

FROM LE CROISIC it was my intention to cross Brittany via the River Vilaine, which would take me as far as Rennes, and then on to Dinan by the Canal a'Ille Rance, and the rest of the way by the tidal River Rance.

On the 1st of June, after first taking some petrol on board, I left Le Croisic for the estuary of the Vilaine, eight miles to the north-east.

It was a sunny day with a brisk wind which threw up small white horses over a grey-blue sea. It was plain sailing until I got to Point du Halguen, less than a mile from the river. Here the water shallows, and over a large area there is six feet or less at low tide. The wind blowing against a strong current produced horrible steep seas, and when I tried to go about, to clear a submerged rock which I had noticed on the chart, the *Nova*, for the first time in her life refused to turn. I had to keep straight on, and hauling in the mainsail until it was as tight as a board, and sailing as close to the wind as possible, I had a bad few minutes, feeling sure in my mind that we would strike. However, nothing happened and I rounded the dangerous corner, bringing the wind nearly astern of me. The tide was now rushing up the river, and with these two forces helping me on my way the *Nova* quickly swept past some oyster flats into calmer water. In places the river narrowed between white chalky cliffs and then suddenly widened without warning where deep creeks cut into the side.

Rounding a curve in the river like a homing pigeon, I had an unpleasant surprise waiting for me. Stretched right across the water was a floating bridge, held in place by a cobweb of heavy wire hawsers. As quickly as my startled wits would allow, I downed the mainsail and swung on the outboard. Luckily it started at once, and when only a couple of yards away from an iron pontoon, I turned with the engine full on, slowly forging back against the tide. This happened opposite La Roche Barnard, which lies about ten miles up the river.

I tied up to a buoy, and then, when the tide was high, moved over alongside a grass covered quay near a ruined windmill. Following a footpath I walked up to the bridge to try to find a loophole. On each side was a guard-house which controlled the single-line traffic. I said to the man inside, "Is it possible for a small boat to get through?" He shook his head and curtly replied, "I do not understand you," so I crossed the bridge to try the man in the other guard-house. Here I had better luck, for he said, "For a boat not more than a metre above the water and two metres wide, you can get through this side at half-tide, but remember to do it when the water flows towards the sea."

Just before night settled over the land, I had both masts lashed down on the cabin top, and ventured the loop hole in the floating bridge. Going very slowly, I edged over to the opposite bank, scraped under the wire hawser, beneath a sloping runway to the first pontoon with an inch to spare, under more hawsers the other side, and I was through. I was as pleased as a rabbit which had found a hole in a garden wire-netting fence. For the night I tied up to a buoy near the ruins of a bridge which, before the Germans blew it up, crossed the river at a height of a hundred feet.

As soon as I noticed the tide turn upstream, I set off with it, having a fixed idea in my head that sooner or later I would have to turn back, for an old man had told me that river traffic had ceased since the floating pontoon bridge had been put across.

The first part of the journey was lovely. The river wound round steep escarpments, tall trees in full leaf grew everywhere a hold could be found. Ferns and lichens splashed the brown rocks with green. Nearer Redon I entered a flat plain and could see nothing but the muddy sides of the river; this gave way to tall reeds which narrowed the breadth to the size of a small trout stream. At this juncture it began to rain in torrents, and to make matters worse the river branched. The way I took dwindled into a reedy swamp. Stopping the outboard and using an oar I turned the boat round with difficulty, for the keel was touching the oozy bottom, then went back the way I had come. When I reached the fork again, I spotted two men rowing a heavy boat with a beam stuck up at an angle from the bow, and dangling from its top was a large circular net on a metal frame.

I shouted, "How do I get to Redon?" They started "lefting" and "righting" till I stopped them in despair and said, "If you are also going to Redon I will give you a tow and you can tell me the way." This idea pleased them immensely. Whether they had intended to go to Redon or not, a tow would be very welcome. With one man standing on the bow of their cumbersome boat, and one telling me which turn to take, we carried on among the reeds, soon passing houses on one side with access to the water cut through the pestilent rushes.

We stopped in front of an unusual barrage having three iron shutters which rested on the river bed. A crowd gathered when I tied up to a broken-down quay in front of the barrage. One man told me it was years since a foreign yacht had passed that way. "Ah," he added with a wistful note, "this waterway is finished."

When the tide made the water level on both sides of the barrage, a man came and said he would raise one shutter to let me through if I wished. I did wish, but it took nearly half an hour for an electric motor to raise the heavy iron shutter to a sufficient height to let me through.

One of the men in charge of the barrage said its main use was for flood control. I gave him and his mate as much as I could spare for a tip and then entered calm tideless water, tying up to a derelict barge with broken deck.

At Redon the Canal Nantes á Brest crosses the Vilaine, and at one time, particularly during the Napoleonic era, this town must have been a hive of industry. Now, though a few barges still use the canal, the stone quays look deserted.

I slept long and deeply, having peace, quiet, and a worry-free mind. The sun was above the house tops before I went shopping, returning to the boat laden with fresh vegetables. My next job was to get water; I could not find a street hydrant and entered an open warehouse. No one was about, so I wandered to the back, found a water-tap, filled the bottle, with furtive glances over my shoulder, and then, still without seeing anyone, stole out. They must be honest, trusting people in Redon.

The Vilaine has fourteen barrages across it to make it navigable as far as Rennes, ninety miles from Redon. While still in the outskirts of

Redon the river looked just like a canal, being narrow and tree-lined with a tow-path running alongside. When ten to fifteen miles on my way the river widened and looked what it was, a river twisting and turning through lovely rural country, where cows lifted their heads to look for the cause of the unusual humming sound coming from their drinking water; spotting me, they gave me a fixed stare until I was out of sight round a bend.

Noticing that I was out of matches, I stopped at a delightful village, buying strawberries at sixpence a pound and a bottle of cream for a shilling, as well as matches. The strawberries and cream were delicious but the matches were a poor buy. Each lit with a bang and then slowly burned along half an inch of sulphur, filling the cabin with sulphur fumes and stinging my eyes and nostrils.

While enjoying to the full my idyllic pastoral surrounding, I was jerked back to the worries of the world when the *Nova* grounded to a sudden standstill on a gravel bank. I tried the depth of water all round and found several inches less than the draft of the *Nova*. It was a difficult job to get going again, but sustained effort of oar and outboard, coupled with rocking the boat to grind a channel for the keel, got us free.

After passing through the first lock, a very primitive affair, I grounded again, but this time I was going slowly and got clear more easily. The river was living up to its name, but it was easy to forget its villainous nature while it remained so beautiful. In the evening I tied up to an overhanging branch of an oak tree, cut off from the outside world by a bower of green. Only an occasional croak of a frog broke the absolute silence of the night. I awoke in the green world, for the sun was shining through the leaves.

A new phase of the river revealed itself that day. It curled round grey rocky cliffs with purple heather growing in every crevice, or past steep slopes covered with trees. In the bright sunlight, white and yellow lilies glowed in abundance among the water weeds. The clear water had the brown colour of a moorland peat stream, which showed off to its full advantage the electric blue of the busy kingfishers darting about. One of these kept me company for several miles, dashing ahead in thirty-yard hops. Anxious moorhens, mothering black fluffy chicks did not like my intrusion into their sphere. Grey herons, too, I disturbed; they rose

M

ponderously with their huge wings flapping slowly, and circled round overhead until I had passed.

As I neared Rennes, all the river's beauty faded away and it became foul with sewage and its green banks dulled as if they too shrank away from the pollution. Rennes, a large town with many solid looking buildings in it, was a good shopping centre. From its noisy vegetable market, pleasant smelling and cheery, I purchased enough to last me for the next leg, and from the Monoprix cheap butter and cheese.

The town is cut in two by the Vilaine, which is kept in its place by high walls. The Canal du Rance joins it by means of a double lock. Town life after a spell in lovely country had no charm for me, and after I had been pestered by a ragged beggar for an hour, a young lady opened the lock for me and I entered the canal. For a while I passed through suburbs where children shouted and ran, then the houses disappeared and once more life was pleasant.

The canal is rapidly falling into ruin, and in places the sides have collapsed into the water, and rushes have crept nearer and nearer the centre. The bridges, so well constructed, and with an ornamented "N" gracing the centre, showed that Napoleon's workers built them to last. They would gladden the eye of any stonemason.

Under an avenue of tall trees I came up to an isolated lock. I was greeted like a prodigal son. Water was obtained from a well by willing hands, and just when I was going to leave the man said, "If you please, will you come to the house for a glass of our home-made cider?" After I agreed with thanks he led the way in. In a biggish room, dirty, with a bed in the corner, I was seated on a chair in front of a bare-board table, and given a glass of cider. It was pleasant and refreshing. The lock-keeper was gnarled and ugly; his wife, I must confess, was a shrewish hag, but these two had produced two pretty daughters, one aged thirteen, the other six. The older one was very fond of music, but, said her mother, "We cannot afford to send her to study; she will have to work on a farm till she finds a man." I appreciated their kindness to me, leaving some pipe tobacco for the man, chocolate for the girls and a tin of sweet milk for the wife.

The next two days I was greatly troubled with weed in the propeller. The only warning I had were sprays of leaves floating in odd spots right across the waterway, but these had strong ropey stems firmly fixed on the bottom, which wrapped like a ball of wool round the propeller. In places I could only manage fifty yards at a time before stopping and cutting them off with a penknife. Tying a long line to the bow I towed the *Nova* through the worst patches. Hard work!

Approaching Dinan, a curve was passed, and a very tall viaduct lay ahead, linking the two ports of the town which are built on opposing hills. A crowd of young boys waved to me just before passing under. Then as I emerged on the other side I heard "plop," "plop," "plop." The young devils were bombing me with stones, but by prompt avoiding action I dodged them. A stone dropped from that height would hurt if it had landed on my head. I shook my fist at them, but thought it must have been fun for them.

It rained all night, bringing to mind that England was not far away. Grey skies and a thin drizzle greeted me in the morning. Trouble soon started, for less than half a mile from Dinan I ran smack on a mud bank. When I tried to push off with the oar, its blade sank, without much effort, as far as the level of the water. Releasing the engine, and swivelling it at right angles to the boat did not do anything but over-heat the motor, so I went below to have a cup of coffee and think it over. It looked as if in this case I would have to have a tow to pull off, but knew this would cost money, of which there was very little in the kitty. Feeling very despondent, I returned on deck, and noticed the boat had not lifted on the mud, but was floating as high as she normally did. Fixing the outboard to push dead ahead, I started it and opened the throttle as far as it would go. The *Nova* moved a couple of feet forward and then stopped again. This time I knew what to do, and ran back and forth across the cabin top, thus making the keel push away the mud on each side, then on with the engine again. The *Nova* finally slid into deeper water an hour later.

Many times I was unsure of the channel on the way to the final lock which joins up the canal with the river, for there were a couple of artificial lakes to cross, and the leading marks were difficult to follow. For the rest of the way I proceeded with caution, sounding every few yards with a pole. In many places there was less than four feet of water, but finally I reached the lock without touching the bottom.

The tide was out, and only a trickle of water ran down the curling channel, which cut deeply amid pale grey wastes of mud. The lock-keeper, a friendly soul, sat with me on the edge of the lock, where fishing enthusiasts were catching tiddlers, and rolled cigarettes from my pipe tobacco. "My friend," he said, "life is not what it was, the Germans corrupted our children, and boats no longer use the canal; where will it all end? This tobacco is very strong and makes me dizzy."

The tide began to rise, and mud flats slowly disappeared, and at 4 o'clock we were allowed to go through.

The River Rance at high tide is like a boa constrictor after it has swallowed half a dozen sheep. It narrows between rocky gorges then opens up into large lakes where the wind produces a nasty chop. However, it was not difficult to navigate and I brought up for the night by tying up to a steamer buoy off St. Servan, quite close to St. Malo. I was up again at 5 a.m. and entered St. Malo through the lock which is capable of taking large ships and in which the *Nova* was dwarfed to a ridiculous size.

Once tied up securely to a quay beside the castellated granite wall of the town, the masts were put up, ropes sorted out, and all made ready for the last sea voyage before home.

At the end of World War Two little remained of St. Malo but its encircling wall. Inside, the rebuilding is almost completed. Tall, square, and all granite-faced, the houses are a credit to the architects and craftsmen. Many artistically decorated shop windows lure the sterling and dollar visitors.

Out of the three days spent in St. Malo, one was almost entirely devoted to the customs. The trouble arose because I had two *Laisses Passez*, and according to the regulations such a thing was impossible. It had come about because I obtained a new one for going through the Vilaine at St. Nazaire and the customs at Bordeaux had failed to collect or stamp my old one. Back and forth we went to various offices. People were "called over the coals" by long distance phone. We paid a visit to the Southern Railway Office to get an interpreter to explain to me the enormity of having two *Laisses Passez*.

Another day I was delighted to hear several men speaking in broad Lancashire. They were busy, looking after crates of live pigeons being unloaded from a British ship. Going up to one of them wearing a cloth cap, I said, "Good morning, can you tell me what's going to happen to these pigeons?" He replied, "They will be sent to various parts of

Northern France, and then released at a certain time, it's a sport in England, you know." Thinking perhaps I was speaking English with a foreign accent, I hastened to tell him I knew a little about pigeon racing and that he was speaking to a fellow countryman.

"I have never seen so many, how many birds are there here?" I asked.

"About 40,000, which will fill thirty-one railway trucks," he replied. "Few people realize the size of the sport in England, or that the Queen is a patron," he concluded proudly.

Though it was the 13th of the month I left St. Malo for Jersey at 8 a.m. in a light but drenching rain. Seeing that it was the 13th and I did not want to be wrecked on the last stages of my voyage, I was particularly careful about navigation. I had to go round the dreaded Minquiers and allow for the strong tides in the Gulf of St. Malo, where the currents are strong as the rise and fall is upwards of thirty feet. However, the passage was made without mishap and in the evening when the wind faded the outboard took me safety into St. Helier, where I was briskly handled by keen officials.

It would have been nice to spend a day or two in Jersey, but with England, home and beauty waiting so near I left St. Helier next morning for Guernsey, a short hop taking only six and a half hours and devoid of trouble, apart from being bounced about in the tide race of La Corbiere. Sark, with its rocks and cliffs glowing in the afternoon sun, tried to allure me but failed.

In St. Peter Port, Guernsey, I was very generously treated, and a great event took place. Mr. Le Pellier, a well-known lawyer in Guernsey, took me to his home, filled up the bath with hot water, and left me soaking in it for an hour. It was my first proper bath for over a year.

Gloomy weather kept me two days in this hospitable port, but on the 17th June I left for the Isle of Wight, ninety miles to the north-north-east. The tide helped until I passed Casquets, whose jagged teeth-like rocks have devoured many a fine sailing ship in the days before modern aids to navigation had been invented.

Throughout the night twilight never completely disappeared, but it was cold in spite of being the middle of June. Fortunately, a light north-west wind kept us jogging along and at 4 in the morning St. Alban's light rose above the horizon and started blinking at me.

The tide began to run to the west, and the wind was only just strong enough to keep me stationary with the coast. The sun mounted and began to warm my chilled body, the tide slackened, stopped, then turned eastwards, and at midday I sailed past the tall knife-like Needles, gleaming white in the sun.

When near the entrance to Yarmouth harbour, a row-boat put out to meet me. It was Stan Smith and his father, welcoming me back home.

FRENCH INLAND WATERWAYS

To wander peacefully through some of France's inland waterways is one of the best and cheapest ways of getting to know that beautiful country. Villages far from the busy arterial roads have that serene, peaceful air which only comes from centuries of planting, weeding and reaping on fertile soil.

The scenery changes so slowly that one does not get that numbed feeling as when speeding through the country in a car with new sights battering the brain in rapid succession.

To the British yachtsman with a motor-boat (large or small) or dinghy with an outboard, the French channel ports of Dunkirk, Bourbourg, Calais, St. Valery, Le Havre and St. Malo give access to canal or river, and all those from Le Havre to Dunkirk link up at varying distances inland.

By entering the Seine at Le Havre and journeying up to Paris it is then possible to take a choice of three routes right through France to the Mediterranean. These three routes have already been mentioned in the text, but perhaps it would be helpful to repeat that the River Marne route goes through the heart of the champagne country!

All three enter the River Saone, which links up with the River Rhone at Lyons. Going down the Rhone necessitates a pilot (cost £15 to £20) and it should be remembered that to return the same way against the current means having powerful motors or a tow to Lyons, which would cost anything from £30 to £100.

To escape that "mean" river, the Rhone, it is possible to cut across France from Cette in the Gulf of Lions to Bordeaux in the Bay of Biscay via the Canal du Midi.

Travel through the French inland waterways is free to foreign yachtsmen but it is necessary to have three documents:

1. A "Permis de Circulation" which is obtainable from the French Government Tourist Office, 179 Piccadilly, London, W.1. It is necessary to state your proposed route and dimensions of craft to be used, not forgetting the height of it above water. No charge for document.

2. A "Permis de Navigation" to certify that your craft is in a fit and proper condition to navigate the inland waterways and is obtainable from the Bureau Veritas, 34 Gt. St. Helens, London, E.C.3. There is a small charge.
3. A "Certificate de Capacite" to prove you are capable of handling your craft and is obtainable from the Yacht and Motor Boat Association, 58 Gordon Square, London, W.C.1.

Besides these three documents you must have a triptyque, obtainable from the Automobile Association or the Royal Automobile Club. Alternatively you can obtain a laissez-passer from the French customs at your port of entry. Don't forget your passport!

In the main canals and rivers, boats with a draft of 6 feet, a maximum beam of 16 feet and overall length of 120 feet are permissible. Maximum possible height above the water is 10 to 11 feet. The Canal du Midi calls for a maximum draft of 5 feet 3 inches.

Going through the locks is hard on the paintwork, and it is advisable to encircle your craft with fenders. Old rubber tyres are very good, but they leave black marks on the paint. When possible keep to the rear of the lock away from the incoming water, which swirls around very violently.

The lock-keepers on the busy canals expect a "tip" but they appeared quite satisfied with a few cigarettes and are always helpful with regard to water and food supplies.

Imray, Laurie, Norie & Wilson Ltd., of St. Ives, Hants, publish a map of France showing most of the navigable rivers and canals. A detailed strip-map of the River Seine from Paris to the sea (Carte de la Seine de Paris a la Mer) is obtainable from Messrs. Sefton, Praed & Co., 67 St. James's Street, London, S.W.1.

SINGLE-HANDED SAILING

NOVA ESPERO

THE *Nova Espero* was designed by Stanley Smith and his brother Colin, in June, 1949, as a small ocean cruiser. She was built in an underground basement of an old chapel at Halifax, Nova Scotia, and measures 15 feet 11 inches on the waterline, and 20 feet in overall length. The beam is 6 feet 3 inches, and the draught 2 feet 10 inches. Her tonnage is slightly over one. No inside ballast is carried, but she has a long fin keel with an 800-pound iron casting along the bottom.

In the design a fairly full fore-section was aimed at in order to help carry the water supply forward of the living space, and to lift the boat quickly when bucking the last sharp curl of a big sea. An easy, rather flat run under water was designed to give the boat a seagull-like sit "on" instead of "in" the water and to allow her to plane forward on "white water." A long fin keel, not too deep, with the weight of iron distributed along a considerable length was designed to give additional longitudinal strength, to ease the violence when pitching, to provide a long plane of lateral resistance in order to reduce any tendency towards restless wavering off course, and to bring down to a minimum the work of the helmsman. Clincher construction was adopted because of its great strength for weight, each "land" representing an unbroken series of stringers. It also provides a partial interruption to the swish of water in the bilge and, very important, curbs the persistent film of water which runs up over a smooth topside, catches in the breeze and rains down upon all on deck.

During the first transatlantic voyage the *Nova Espero* had no cabin, but merely a dinghy upturned over the cockpit to form a shelter, but for her second ocean voyage the cabin was constructed, with three main purposes in mind: reserve buoyancy, comfort with utility, and strength. It was built up from the topsides, and the timbers extended correspondingly. The step down to the foredeck was about 9 inches deep and kept nearly all green water and spray from coming aft, except, of course, when punching into short, steep seas.

Two bunks were built in and the coamings round the cockpit were heightened on the second voyage, being on average 5 inches from the deck. Other ideas incorporated in the design were watertight bulkheads fore and aft and, rather unusual, a tiller under cover of the deck, to lessen the chances of exposure. Lockers along the sides were provided to allow a fairly clear space in which to live, to reduce a little the violence of a small boat's rolling and to minimize the risk of the man below getting thrown disastrously from one side to the other.

For her second voyage the *Nova Espero* was altered from sloop to yawl rig. The mainmast was short (18 feet) and stubby, and it was stepped in a tabernacle on the cabin deck, reinforced by a big seven-eighth-inch bonded-ply frame, which carries the weight down beyond the turn of the bilge. The mast was stepped on deck because if by some sudden strain the shrouds parted, it could be regained in one whole piece, not leaving a section below decks as usually happens when a mast is stepped on the keelson. It also gave extra cabin space.

The sail area is 200 square feet, and the mainsail is sliding gunter to allow quick dowsing of weight aloft and to lessen the risk of losing the mast if rolled over in big seas. All standing rigging is designed to be spliced exactly the same lengths to allow a quick interchange if necessity arises, and all halliards and sheets are of one standard size for the same reason.

The sails were made of strong Egyptian cotton with the seams on the main and mizen running up and down, so that a tear in a panel would only go from seam to seam instead of right across the sail as would happen with horizontal seams. The luff wires were stainless steel. There was only a single deep reef, for, after all, when the wind increases at sea a small boat must not dally with half measures. Battens hamper the rapid handling of a sail, so these were eliminated. A high foot for the foresail was provided to avoid the danger of the sail being burst by a heavy sea.

The rigging was kept as simple as possible with sheaves and pulleys large enough for the ropes to slip through easily. The halliards lead to jam cleats aft of the cabin-top, and the main and jib could be lowered in a matter of seconds from the cockpit—very useful in squalls!

For *Nova Espero*'s third voyage the boat was not altered in any way for single-handed sailing. She was given a hasty coat of paint and there was

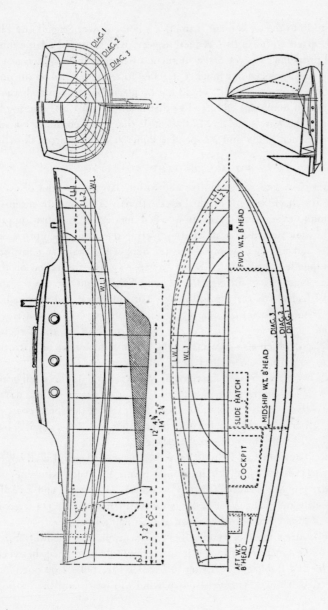

NOVA ESPERO: Length overall, 20 ft.; Length waterline, 15 ft. 11 in.; Beam, 6 ft. 3 in.; Draft, 2 ft. 10 in.

an addition to the equipment, namely a 4 horse-power Seagull 102 Plus model, fitted with a 3 to 1 reduction gear, which turned a large four-bladed propeller. I never had a moment's worry with it. When in use the engine was placed in a bracket attached to a wooden pad on the port side of the transom stern (it could not be placed in the centre because of the mizen bumpkin) and fixed so that it would not turn, steering by the use of the *Nova*'s rudder. In the canals the petrol consumption was 11.2 miles per gallon and its speed 5 knots at three-quarter throttle.

EQUIPMENT AND STORES

Charts nowadays are expensive and to buy large-scale ones of every mile to the Black Sea (my original destination) was beyond my means—you cannot take every precaution when money is in short supply. Instead I took two small-scale charts covering the entire Mediterranean (2158 A and B), then as my route lay between Corsica and Sardinia I had a detailed chart of that notorious area (1189) and relied on the Mediterranean charts through the Messina Straits, but for Greece and beyond I had charts for the following: Gulf of Patras and approaches (1676), Gulf of Corinth, Corinth Canal, Aiyion Bay (1600), Calymnos and Cos Islands, large-scale (3925) Northern sheet of the Grecian Archipelago, which also gave the Straits of Galipoli and Sea of Marmara (2836 B), one small-scale chart of the Black Sea (2214).

When my plans changed I arrived at Malta using only the small-scale chart of the Mediterranean, but there I obtained charts for the north coast of Africa, Sicily, Sardinia, Corsica and parts of the south coast of France, all free of charge, for they were stamped "cancelled," but were obsolete only in minor technicalities.

For the Bay of Biscay, Brittany, and the Channel Islands, I used large-scale charts all the time, kindly loaned to me by Major Kitchener of Bermuda. For navigation I had only a compass, a sextant, and a really good deck watch. The *Nova Espero* is too small to tow a log. I tried it once, and found it slowed her down at least half a knot.

After hearing tales of sudden fierce storms in the Mediterranean I carried a sea-anchor, 27 inches in diameter (only used once, between Marseilles and Bonifacio). "Lying to" under bare poles I do not like, having tried it once. You drift down wind too much and the motion is worse.

Two anchors were carried, a 50-pound Navy type which proved too heavy to handle easily, and not very efficient, and a 25-pound fisherman type, which was easy to handle and had excellent holding power given plenty of scope. I had two manilla warps, one 2 inches in diameter and 25 fathoms long—too much and very heavy, the other was 1½ inches diameter and 10 fathoms long. The latter was easier to handle, but once proved to be too short. Fifteen to twenty fathoms should be plenty for a boat the size of *Nova*. There are no winches aboard the boat, and no chain was carried. Three working sails, mizen, mainsail and jib, an ancient trysail, and a spinnaker were all the sails I carried. There was no use nor space for any others, but I took the precaution of carrying sail needles and thread, though never used them. The jib sheets were single-part and led through a "dead-eye" on the cabin top. The main sheet was led through two blocks giving a two to one advantage.

For halliards, both the jib and mizen were single-part. The main and jib halliards led from snatch blocks at the foot of the mast nearly back to the cockpit, which enabled me to raise and lower all sails without leaving the tiller. All sheets and halliards were 1½-inch sisal.

My water I carried in two 10-litre wicker bottles. This would last me a week to ten days.

HANDLING

When alone at sea it greatly helps the daily mileage if the boat can be made to sail herself while eating or sleeping. Slocum's boat, the *Spray*, was incredibly good at this, but Ann Davidson's and Allcard's boats were just the reverse and made for longer more arduous passages. Our boat is in between the two extremes, for she will sail by herself with the wind forward of the beam under mizen, main and jib with the tiller lashed to suit the strength of wind. However, with jib and mizen cnly she will sail herself with the wind abeam or forward of the beam, and the tiller free, adjusting the course by slightly freeing or tightening the mizen sheet. Once I made the *Nova* steer herself with the wind on the quarter, using the spinnaker instead of jib, no mainsail and the mizen fairly loose. The wind was very steady on this occasion, which is perhaps why I was never able to repeat the performance.

When the boat was sailing herself I got plenty of sleep during the day and kept awake (or tried to!) during the night. When it was a case of having to steer and keep on course the routine was different. I would keep at the tiller as long as possible, getting food and hot drinks by steering with my foot while I was grabbing about in the food locker just inside the cabin. Gybes and unexpected tacks were not unknown during these manoeuvres!

A day and a night was as much as I could take, and when the first light of day came again and the boat could be seen I would, if the wind was dead astern, turn the boat into and heave-to with the jib aweather, the main and mizen hard in, and tiller free, then sleep for an hour or two—delightful! If the wind was on the quarter then I would make her sail herself as near to my course as possible, though at times she's been as much as 60 degrees off course while I rested.

The famous single-handers like Slocum (he always comes first), Pidgeon, Gerbault, Allcard and Ann Davidson went alone for a variety of reasons. Some found it impossible to find a really compatible companion, others like Gerbault really preferred their own company, or like Ann Davidson set out to prove something either to themselves or to other people.

Long ago while working in Bermuda and also when I set out on a single-handed ill-fated voyage from Nova Scotia to England, I found that it was easier on my nerves to voyage alone, with the exception of the time I crossed from London to New York, with Stan Smith, but then he's an exception himself!

Night is the time when things can become eerie, especially when the wind begins to rise and howl in the rigging, and sudden breakingcr ests alongside make you jump. Then you begin to wonder whether you should tuck in a reef, or whether you are being a sissy. Long before morning comes you have come to the conclusion you are just a silly fool and when you get back home you will stay there for ever. But, oh, let the night be gentle, and the wind a cool caress, with the stars above like yellow diamonds on dark blue velvet, then all earthly things seem to vanish and you gently glide through a timeless dimensionless universe, conscious only that you are on the brink of understanding its profound mystery. (You never do!)

Making a landfall single-handed has a charm all of its own, and is very exciting, though I fear it has much to do with a swelling ego.

The enemies of pleasureable sailing, cold, rain, unmanageable winds and ill-health, do terrible things to the morale, and I've always found it pays to set sail when the weather seems set fine, and I am feeling well physically. At sea I always did things the easiest possible way. For instance, when reefing I would lower the mainsail completely and tie in the reef sitting down, and did not attempt to do it partially lowered and raving about like a mad thing.

Setting the spinnaker was my hardest job. I would put the boat before the wind then (having no spinnaker halliard), lower the jib, after which it meant mad scrambles to and from foredeck to tiller, for the yacht would only stay on her course a matter of seconds. Sometimes I would try with the boat lying in the wind, but as often as not the spinnaker would fill before I was ready and carry its sheets up into the air and then collapse into the sea. I never did find an easy way of putting up that spinnaker alone!

Whenever I left the cockpit and whenever I remembered I tied a rope round my waist, the other end of which was made fast to the foot of the mast. The fear of falling overboard is often present when alone.

FOOD

If it is necessary to economize when in the Mediterranean, do not eat out, but go to the open-air market early in the morning and buy your vegetables, fruit and, if you can afford it, meat, and cook your own meals aboard. Vegetables (in season), wine and tobacco seem to be the only cheap items found in the shops of the Mediterranean. Meat, butter and cheese are higher in price than in Britain. Perhaps the trouble lies in the rate of exchange. At the time of writing 100 francs equals two shillings, but it had less purchasing power in France than two shillings here. Before leaving port I would buy enough vegetables to last me a week, chiefly potatoes, carrots and dried split green peas, a few loaves of bread, a kilo of over-ripe bananas, obtained at a reduced price, 200 grammes of cheese, and two litres of paraffin for the stove. After topping up my water bottles and carefully stowing half a gallon of wine, I was all ready for the next leg. I carried on board tinned butter, tea, Marmite and Bovril, all of which I had bought in fairly large quantities in Britain.

After leaving Yarmouth, I.O.W., and voyaging about 5,000 miles in just over a year, I only spent £60 in cash, and felt very fit at the end of it all.

PEOPLE

In every country I visited I met with much hospitality and kindness. I did learn one important lesson, never to judge a man by my own standards, but to attempt to do so by the standard of his own environment. I received as much friendliness from the poor as the wealthy, and far less inhibitions and reserve than one meets in these damp isles!

MEDITERRANEAN WEATHER

In May, June, July and August it is possible to sail about without having to fight a really bad mistral. By the end of October, most of the numerous Italian auxiliary sailing vessels lay up for the winter, for then one can expect fierce storms to blow up almost without warning. Winter mistrals are notorious, especially in the Gulf of Lions. They are caused by a belt of high pressure over Northern France and a trough of low in the Mediterranean. Cold dry air built up in the high pressure rushes down the Rhone Valley, which has a funnelling effect, to the low area in the south. This bitter wind is so powerful it has been known to blow trains off their tracks and devastate shipping in the Gulf of Lions. There is not much warning. The barometer sags a little, the night dew disappears, and then you must stand by for trouble.